**NORTH EAST of SCOTLAND LIBRARY SERVICE**
14 Crown Terrace, Aberdeen

DONALDSON, Gordon

Sir William Fraser

6.

# SIR WILLIAM FRASER

*The Man and His Work*

Gordon Donaldson

The Edina Press
Edinburgh

THE EDINA PRESS

1 Albyn Place,
Edinburgh EH2 4NG


*First published 1985*


ISBN   0   905695   11   9

F2
FRA
6.
969661

Printed in Scotland
by
Office Printing Services, Edinburgh

# CONTENTS

## ILLUSTRATIONS

# INTRODUCTION

Fraser's fifty or so volumes on the histories of between twenty and thirty of the leading noble and landed families of Scotland may well seem in themselves a more than ample memorial to the industry of one man – and a man who, during most of the years when he was compiling those books, was also officially employed on the staff of the Register House. But those who have had occasion, in the course of their own historical work, to turn to the contents of Scottish charter rooms or to investigate or verify points in the genealogy of notable Scottish families are frequently aware of coming on Fraser's tracks. Apart from the prints of the many peerage cases in which he gave evidence and the published Reports of the Historical Manuscripts Commission, Fraser's wide-ranging activities resulted in the existence of unpublished lists and inventories of muniments and of countless bundles of documents still bearing signs that he once examined them.

This being so, the materials for an account of Fraser's work lay scattered in castles and mansions throughout the length and breadth of the country. In recent years, thanks to the transmission of so many private collections to the Register House and to the surveying of so many more by the National Register of Archives (Scotland), the task of finding information which throws light on Fraser's operations has become easier. Even so, however, I would not claim anything like completeness for what I have brought together in the following pages, because much more may still lurk undiscovered or at any rate unnoted. At the same time, it is perhaps unlikely that additional information would do more than multiply instances of Fraser's operations or add further illustrations of his methods.

His Grace the Duke of Buccleuch readily gave me permission to use material from his Muniments, deposited in the Scottish Record Office. I am much indebted to members of the Record Office staff who have been so kind in drawing my attention to Fraser material which they have come across. I have also to acknowledge help from

the staffs of the National Library of Scotland, Edinburgh
University Library and the Lyon Office, Mr Douglas Moffat
of Tods, Murray and Jamieson (agents for the Fraser
Trustees) and Mr Murdo MacDonald, Archivist of Argyll
and Bute District Council, all of whom enabled me to have
access to relevant records and papers.

At least four portraits of Fraser are known. (1) A
painting by William Crabb, dated 1869, is in Edinburgh
University. A few years ago Dr Cadoux, Senior Lecturer
in Ancient History, had this portrait photographed and
one copy was placed in his Department and another in
the Scottish History Department. (2) An engraving dated
1886 is reproduced in the Scottish History Society volume
of *Fraser Papers*. (3) There are several reproductions
in the Fraser Homes of a portrait showing Fraser in full
dress as a K.C.B. (4) A signed photograph of 1887 is
reproduced in this volume. (5) A beautifully detailed small
oil painting, size 8" x 6", apparently based on the
photograph of 1887, signed 'Tos. Faed', is in The
Merchants' Hall, Hanover Street, Edinburgh.

# CHAPTER 1

## EARLY YEARS AND PRIVATE LIFE

William Fraser came of the stock of farmers and craftsmen in the Mearns, but, although there had been Fraser families in that district and in adjoining Aberdeenshire for centuries, his own ancestry derived from Banffshire, and that, he would no doubt note, took his lineage a little nearer to the estates of the leading Fraser family, that of Lovat. He could trace as far back as his great-grandfather, John, who was 'said to be "of the Frasers of Lovat" ' and apparently came from the parish of Kirkmichael in Banffshire, which includes the mountainous country around Tomintoul and part of the valley of the Avon. But by the time John married Jean (or Janet) Carmichael, on 18 July 1738, he was farming in the parish of Aberlour, in the less forbidding lands of lower Strathspey. The couple had two daughters, whose names, Anne and Clementina, might suggest a lingering attachment to the Stewart line, whose last sovereign had been Queen Anne and whose male representative, the Old Pretender, had married Clementina Sobieski; but neither of those Christian names was altogether rare in Scotland at the time. They also had a son, William, baptized on 5 October 1746, who learned the mason craft and in his early twenties made his way to the vicinity of Stonehaven, where he worked on the erection of a new steading at Cowie, just north of that town. He married Christian, daughter of James Young, tenant of the Mill of Cowie. Their large family included James (baptized on 28 July 1786), who, like his father, was a mason. In 1815 he married Ann, daughter of James Walker, tenant of the farm of Elfhill of Fetteresso, about five miles from Stonehaven, and his wife Jean Aitershank(s), and the couple settled at Links of Arduthie, on which part of Stonehaven was later built. Their children were William, born 18 February 1816, John, born 31 July 1818, and Ann, born 29 August 1820. [1] (When Fraser died, his estate included some land and houses in Stonehaven, lying between Mary Street and Robert Street, in the estate of Arduthie, and this may have been his childhood home; it was sold for £610, which by the standards of the time

suggests that it was fairly substantial.)[2]
    William was educated at a private school in Stone-
haven kept by the Rev. Charles Michie, who had
graduated M.A. at Marischal College in 1810 but has not
been identified in any of the standard lists of clergy;
possibly, whatever his denomination, he never had a
congregational charge but spent his life teaching. On 23
August 1830 the fourteen-year-old William began a five-
year apprenticeship with Messrs. Brand and Burnett,
Solicitors, Stonehaven. An account of his life adds:'During
these years he made many friends of his own age, with
whom, after he left Stonehaven, he kept up a correspondence dignified and precocious on both sides. He also seems
to have been caught by the prevailing excitement about
the Reform Bill of 1832, for one of his most cherished
possessions was a banner with an appropriate inscription,
apparently home-made, which he had carried in a pro-
cession to celebrate the passing of that measure and
welcome the new heaven and new earth which, it was
understood, this alteration of electoral machinery would
soon produce'.[3]
    Fraser's mother died in 1821, when he was five, and
his brother John died shortly afterwards. James Fraser,
the father, died in 1834 at the age of forty-seven, so that
William, now eighteen, and his sister Ann, aged thirteen,
were orphans. 'That the boy had commended himself to his
employers, and that the family circumstances were somewhat narrow, is evidenced by the terms of a letter of
sympathy from Mr Brand [the senior partner in the firm
which employed Fraser], with a gift of £5, and by the
lad's reply. Even in those early days it is plain that Sir
William carefully prepared his letters and preserved the
drafts'.[4]
    Fraser went to Edinburgh in December 1835, when he
was barely twenty, and joined the firm of Hill and Tod,
W.S., with whom he remained for four years. He continued
his education, by attending classes, including Scots Law
and Conveyancing, at the University, and by being
coached in French in 1838.[5] From 1840 to 1848 he was
with Warren Hastings Sands, W.S., who had been Solicitor
to the Teind Court since 1825. During this period he began
to practice on his own account, partly in connection with
peerage claims and other cases where historical knowledge
was useful. He also served in these years as clerk to two
notable lawyers. One was Charles Baillie, later Lord
Jerviswoode, who was advocate depute 1844-6 and 1852,
sheriff of Stirling 1853-8, solicitor general and lord
advocate 1858. The other was that expert in Scottish legal
and constitutional history Cosmo Innes, who had been
advocate depute in 1833 and was sheriff of Elgin and

Nairn from 1840 to 1852. Fraser moved on in 1848 to employment by John Gibson, a W.S. who had acted for Sir Walter Scott in his later years and had played a key role in framing the complicated arrangements necessitated by Sir Walter's financial collapse. In 1851 Fraser joined Gibson's son in the firm of Gibsons and Fraser, W.S., and in February of that year he was admitted a member of the Society of Solicitors before the Supreme Court.[6]

Throughout his early years in Edinburgh Fraser maintained a regular correspondence with friends in the Mearns. From such letters as have been preserved it is plain that away in Edinburgh, and steadily climbing the professional ladder, William maintained a keen and kindly interest not merely in his own kinsfolk but in his native place and its people generally, and was always ready to help in every deserving object – and some undeserving ones – that were commended to his notice. Among his correspondents was his uncle John Dickson, who had married James Fraser's sister Jean and farmed at Alpity, in Arbuthnott parish. It seems that when events in the Church of Scotland were taking the shape which led to the Disruption of 1843, William Fraser was sympathetic to the party opposed to patronage and was a great admirer of Thomas Guthrie, minister of St John's in Edinburgh, who seceded to join the Free Church, but his decision to remain faithful to the 'Auld Kirk' was due to some extent to the influence of his uncle John: 'The hard-headed old gentleman, for many years an elder and Session Treasurer of the parish of Fetteresso, did not regard the constitution of the Church as perfect; but he did not think that a Disruption was the best way to put things right, and he made this very clear to his nephew'.[7]

'In those days the remuneration of a law clerk depended a good deal on the amount of writing which he did, and Fraser's remarkably fine script was thus of material use in increasing his income. He also for a considerable time kept the business books of his employers, and so developed those orderly and methodical habits that characterised him in such a marked degree. It was his good fortune also to be concerned in various cases requiring antiquarian and, in particular, genealogical research, and he was thus early introduced to those studies in which he became such an expert, and steadily built up that remarkable body of knowledge which made possible his great series of family histories'.[8] This generalisation is possibly all that can be said about Fraser's professional work while he was still in a private office, for his surviving papers throw little light on his activities outside the historical and genealogical fields; in 1849, however, he was engaged in 'The Granton Pier

Business' and was 'under orders to go to London' in connection with it 'if the Edinburgh and North Railway Bill comes on before Easter'.[9]

The Edinburgh and Northern Railway, re-named the Edinburgh, Perth and Dundee, was on the point of beginning to operate the world's first train ferry from Granton to Burntisland, and the Duke of Buccleuch, who owned the harbour, had an interest in the railway company; one can only speculate whether Fraser's association with Buccleuch at this point was at all linked with the subsequent connection, extending over three decades, arising from the study of the history of the ducal family.

In his early years in Edinburgh Fraser lived in lodgings. Apparently for a considerable time he shared quarters at 18 Dundas Street with another law clerk, Archibald Grant, but left there on 29 August 1845, obvious-- ly, because 'Archy' was to be married on 1 September, when Fraser was his 'best man', and he moved to lodgings with Mr and Mrs Finlayson at 9 Queensferry Street, where Alexander Paul joined him. In this period the address 5 Royal Circus was given for Fraser, but that must have been an office. From October 1846 his home was a flat at 11 Forres Street, which he styled 'my own house' but which was rented from James Watson, writer. His office address was now 12 Charlotte Street. He did not leave Forres Street until 1860, when he bought the ground and first floors of 32 Castle Street, with basement and stable. and this remained his home for the rest of his life.[10] The previous occupant was James Cunningham Graham, advocate, whose son Kenneth, author of *The Wind in the Willows*, was born there in 1859, as a plaque affixed to the house reminds the passer-by.

Fraser's sister Anne, his junior by four years. whose arrival in Edinburgh (after the death of their grandmother) he had noted on 27 May 1845 but who did not at first live under the same roof with him, moved into Forres Street to keep house for him there and remained his housekeeper until her death three months before his own.[11] She was supported by a succession of servants. whose names changed from Census to Census: in 1851 Jessie Scott. an Edinburgh girl of 17; in 1861 Harriet Kitchen, an Edinburgh girl of 23; in 1871 Janet Niven and Fanny Cowane, the first a 35-year-old from Edinburgh and the second a 23-year-old from Leith; in 1881 Elizabeth and Jessie Brown, both natives of Edinburgh, the first aged 27 and the second aged 20; in 1891 Helen Miller. 'cook, domestic', aged 33, from Latheron, and Johan MacLennan, 'tablemaid, domestic', aged 21, from Killearn.[12]   Two things are suggested by those simple facts: first, that the household became more affluent and pretentious as the years went by, and second that, despite the bachelor Fraser's reputed disapproval of 'followers' courting his servants, [13] and the fact that they were all unmarried when in his service, the 'turnover' among his staff strongly indicates that they left on marriage. When Fraser died three months after his sister the informant of the death was James MacLeod, described as an 'inmate' of the household, which suggests that he was not a manservant; he should be identified with a James MacLeod who had been one of Fraser's 'office clerks' and probably also with the James MacLeod who was a son of the Rev. Walter MacLeod and brother of John MacLeod, both of whom had worked with Fraser over the years. [14]

Fraser was a member of 'the West Church', otherwise St Cuthbert's, and several times from June 1845 onwards he mentioned that he worshipped there, once (27 October 1861) 'attending the sacrament'.[15] The fact that on one occasion he remarked that he would have to be at St Cuthbert's next day makes it seem likely that he was an elder with duties to perform. In the list of elders there is a William M. Fraser (1879–83), but this seems unlikely to be our man unless there has been an error. [16] On 29 June 1845, after being at St Cuthbert's in the forenoon he was at South Leith Church in the afternoon: as he remarks that 'a stranger preached', he may have been disappointed at not hearing the minister of the parish, but perhaps he was interested mainly in visiting a historic church, the 'restoration' of which was completed three years later.[17] On Fraser's death the funeral was conducted by Dr Wallace Williamson, then minister of St Cuthbert's, and he was buried in the Dean Cemetery. [18] His grave is marked by a monument designed by A.F. Balfour Paul, who was architect of the Fraser Homes.

# CHAPTER 2

## THE REGISTER HOUSE

Fraser's work, perhaps from his first arrival in Edinburgh and certainly as his professional activities developed, meant that he had many contacts with the Scottish national archives in the Register House, and he had shown an appreciation of the claim of that official repository by drawing attention to material which he came on in various collections but which was properly public record. Thus in 1846, when investigating the charters at Marchmont House, he found papers which had belonged to the 1st Earl of Marchmont in his capacity as Chancellor (1696-1702) and he arranged for their transmission to the Register House.[1] Then in 1850, when working in the sheriff clerk's office at Forfar, he discovered volumes of the records of the commissary court of Brechin and reported that they should find a home with similar material in Edinburgh.[2] On the other hand, in 1866-7 he 'recovered for the Duke of Argyll from the Register House a valuable volume of royal letters to the Argyll family', and in such a case he could devote a lot of time to proving the rights of a private owner when he was convinced of their validity, as entries in the account which he subsequently rendered show.[3]

It may not seem surprising that a man with Fraser's interests and experience ultimately found a place on the Register House staff, but it is impossible to be confident as to the considerations which led him in 1852, at the age of thirty-six, to give up full-time private practice for an appointment as Assistant Keeper of the Register of Sasines. The salary of £500, though then a substantial one, is unlikely to have exceeded much, if at all, the actual and prospective rewards of a lucrative and promising practice, but it did offer security and a pension (though as yet without a statutory retiring age). What may have weighed more in Fraser's mind was that he had reason to expect rapid promotion and that he could have ample time to continue private practice, as the office hours were at that time 10-3 on weekdays and 10-12 on Saturdays, perhaps with attendance when necessary on some evenings and from

12 to 2 on Saturdays (By 1870 the hours were 10 to 4 on weekdays and 10 to 12 on Saturdays.)[4] At any rate, Fraser remained on the staff until his retirement forty years later.

At the time of his appointment, the office of Lord Clerk Register, at the apex of the staff structure, was on the way to becoming a mere position of honour, in the hands of Lord Dalhousie, who held it from 1845 to 1860 but from 1847 to 1856 was also Governor General of India and did not draw the Clerk-Register's salary of £1200 when he was in the east. In Dalhousie's successor, however, Sir William Gibson Craig, appointed in 1862, there was once more – for the last time – a 'working' Lord Clerk Register, though for some years he worked gratuitously, pending a decision on the utility and future of his office, which (along with that of Lord Lyon) had been condemned by the Treasury in 1855 as fulfilling 'no function of public importance'. The effective head of the record authority during Dalhousie's tenure was William Pitt Dundas, a son of Robert Dundas of Arniston, who had succeeded the great Thomas Thomson as Deputy Clerk Register in 1841, with a salary of £500. The office of Deputy Keeper of the Records was held jointly by two brothers, George and William Robertson, appointed by Commission in 1829 at £600 each with the proviso that the private searching permitted to them was not to be allowed to their successors. Thus when George died in 1853 and William retired the Treasury appointed George Brown Robertson, son of George, as sole deputy keeper, since all his time would be devoted to official business, and established a searching department with four official searchers at £400 each, an antiquarian searcher at £200 and three clerks. Joseph Robertson ran the Historical Department from 1854 with a salary of £400 and was succeeded by Thomas Dickson in 1867. The Keeper of the Register of Sasines was Alexander Pringle of Whytbank, who was an advocate but had owed his appointment in 1846 to patronage and, when he persuaded Fraser to become Assistant Keeper, may have sought to strengthen his department and possibly led Fraser to expect the succession to the office of Keeper of Sasines. However, when Pringle died in September 1857 it was not Fraser, but John Clerk Brodie of Idvies, W.S., who succeeded. This may have created an unhappy situation, but the personal relations between Fraser and Brodie seem sometimes to have been friendly enough, as letters written by Fraser show. Writing to Brodie in 1870 he begins formally 'Dear Sir' and ends 'I remain yours faithfully', but the tone of the letter is informal and it includes personal details; in another letter of the same year Fraser gives Brodie an account of a fall from a pony when he was staying at Glenferness, Lord Leven's house in Moray; and in 1875, when reporting to Brodie on the success of the Mar Peerage Case, Fraser remarks, 'we have worked very cordially together during these eight anxious years'.[5] George B. Robertson, Deputy Keeper of the Records, died in 1873 and was succeeded next year by John Cockburn Christie, who had been promoted from a position as a searcher in the searching department to the principal keepership of the Register of Deeds.[6]

Changes took place in the structure as well as the personnel of the office in 1879-81. Gibson Craig, Lord Clerk Register, died in 1878 and was succeeded next year by the Earl of Glasgow, who, however, in virtue of an act passed in 1879, was the first of the essentially honorific holders of the office, with no functions in the administration of the records. The Duke of Montrose succeeded Glasgow on his death in 1890. Pitt Dundas resigned as Deputy Clerk Register in 1880, to be succeeded by Roger Montgomerie, who inherited the powers formerly vested in the Lord Clerk Register and also his salary of £1200. On Montgomerie's death next year Sir Stair Agnew was appointed and held the office until 1909. Searching was transferred to the Sasines Department in 1881.

John C. Christie, the Deputy Keeper of the Records, died on 29 August 1880. Roger Montgomerie, the Deputy Clerk Register, at once wrote to the Treasury recommending Fraser, of whom he wrote: 'Mr Fraser has for many years occupied his present position and has an intimate knowledge of all the departments of the Register House. He is a trained lawyer. His abilities are well known and his knowledge of the immense store of records and legal documents which this office contains is great. His appointment would be acceptable to the legal profession and to the public generally'.[7] The appointment was made before the end of September.[8] It was pointed out that as Deputy Keeper of Sasines, with a salary of £500, Fraser was entitled to superannuation but that as Deputy Keeper of the Records, with a salary of £600, he would not be so entitled, and it was agreed that on his final retirement he would carry at least the pension which was his due as Deputy Keeper of Sasines.[9] The salary remained at £600 for Fraser's lifetime.[10]

Already sixty-four on his appointment as Deputy Keeper of the Records, and largely absorbed in his extra-official activities, Fraser was hardly the man to initiate an era of change or development in the Register House, and the twelve years of his tenure were of little significance. There was not even, as might perhaps have been expected, much expansion of the ambitious publications programme which was already under way. The

*Acts of the Parliaments* had been completed in 1875; the first series of the *Register of the Privy Council* had begun in 1877 and the second did not begin until 1899; the *Treasurers' Accounts* had begun in 1877, the *Exchequer Rolls* in 1878. The one series of which publication in effect began in Fraser's time was the *Register of the Great Seal*, of which a folio volume had appeared in 1814 but on which nothing more was done until 1882, from which date there was steady progress. The *Calendar of Documents relating to Scotland* began in 1881, but this was a calendar of material in the English records in London.

It is not clear, either, that Fraser brought any great drive to the other tasks, of arranging the records and providing guides to them. An official *Guide to the Public Records of Scotland* was prepared only in the time of Fraser's successor, Matthew Livingstone. Fraser did indeed sign a memorandum in 1887 regarding a list of admissions of notaries from 1577 to 1709, based on newly discovered material,[11] but it is not clear whether he was personally responsible for this. One would have thought that it would be in tune with his interests to deal with the collection of charters, other documents and seals which had been presented to the office by Cosmo Innes in 1864, but even this task was deferred: as late as 1891 Fraser reported that they had been 'lying in a heap and unarranged'[12] but he had now arranged the 'Innes Charters', amounting to 167 writs.[13]

There were of course more or less routine duties to be performed, and Fraser had at least to attach his signature to statements relating to the organisation of the office. Thus in 1887 he was responsible for explaining to the Queen's and Lord Treasurer's Remembrancer why there had been a decrease in the fees collected by the 'office of the Lord Clerk Register'.[14] In 1887 he signed a memorandum explaining that before 1881 there were four official searchers under the Deputy Keeper of the Records but that searching was then transferred to the Keeper of the Register of Sasines and the searchers and their clerks were added to that keeper's staff.[15] In 1883 an interesting technicality arose in connection with two errors in an extract bond about which Fraser had to write to Crawford and Heron, Writers in Glasgow: 'Since my appointment to my present office, all extracts have been twice collated. Long experience proved to me that single collations were much less accurate than double. This is the first instance in which any mistakes have occurred'. He explained that there was also a mistake in the record volume, but that no alteration could be made in it even if the original bond were transmitted to prove the error. 'It is a rule of office that no alteration can be made in the Record after final transmission'.[16]

It was more characteristic of Fraser to engage in defending the prestige of officers of state. In 1878, when Sir William Gibson Craig, the Lord Clerk Register, died, he wrote to the 9th Marquis of Lothian, who had been Lord Privy Seal for Scotland since 1874 and with whom Fraser had already established friendship through his work on private muniments: 'The office of Lord Register will be kept up, I believe, at the present salary of £1200, which was abolished by Mr Gladstone on the death of Lord Dalhousie in 1860 but restored again in virtue of an act of parliament in 1868'. (Other information, how- ever, is that after a period when Craig worked gratuitous- ly the salary was restored in 1871.) Fraser added that he thought Lord Lothian's own chances of appointment were good, but there were several candidates and it was Lord Glasgow who was appointed. [17] In 1883, writing to another of his noble clients, the Duke of Buccleuch, Fraser alluded to a change which had been made in the entry relating to the Registers and Records of Scotland in Oliver and Boyd's *Edinburgh Almanac*. In 1881 and 1882 the entry had been headed with the name of the Earl of Glasgow, Lord Clerk Register and Keeper of the Signet, and there followed 'Deputy Clerk Register – Stair Agnew, Advocate; Deputy Keeper of the Records – William Fraser. S.S.C.; Curator of Historical Records – T. Dickson.' In 1883 the layout was completely recast, with no mention of Lord Glasgow and headed 'Keeper of the Records of Scotland and Registrar General (Deputy Clerk Register) – Stair Agnew, Advocate'. Fraser put it thus to Buccleuch: 'For many years the Lord Register's name stood in all almanacs as head of the Register House. But this year, without any communication with his lordship, the Deputy struck his name out of Oliver and Boyd's Almanac and substituted his own and a new official name different from Deputy Clerk Register. This was very irregular and has led Lord Glasgow to protest for remedy next year'. [18] The protest was successful, for in 1884 the entry ran: 'Lord Clerk Register and Keeper of the Signet – The Earl of Glasgow; Keeper of the Records of Scotland and Registrar General (Deputy Clerk Register) – Stair Agnew, Advocate;....' The same style was followed until so recently as 1965, com- memorating a victory for Fraser. The sense of propriety which stimulated him on this occasion led him also, about the same time, to complain that in a new appointment of the Historical Manuscripts Commission Lord Lothian was denied his style as Keeper of the Privy Seal of Scotland.[19]

One task which fell to Fraser and which he found extremely congenial was his participation, as Deputy Keeper, in arranging and attending the elections of the sixteen Scottish peers who, in terms of the Treaty of Union, were chosen to sit in the House of Lords. As an election took place not only when a new parliament was proclaimed but also when a vacancy occurred (usually by death), this duty was carried out by Fraser no less than twelve times, at the general elections of 1880, 1886 and 1892 and at by-elections in 1882, 1885 (thrice), 1886 (twice), 1889, 1890 and 1891. The occasions were opportunities for Fraser to maintain his acquaintanceships among the peerage which had come about through his research and writings.

Lord Lothian was Secretary for Scotland from 1886 to 1892, and therefore at the head of Scottish affairs when the office of Clerk Register fell vacant by the death of Lord Glasgow in 1890. Not surprisingly, he asked Fraser, with whom he had come to be on increasingly cordial terms over the years, for his opinion on the appointment of a successor. [20]

Lothian was still secretary when, on 1 April 1892, Fraser became due for retirement 'in virtue of the order in council introducing compulsory retirement on account of age', but Lothian considered it expedient that there should be no change in the record department until after the forthcoming peers' election, 'at which the Deputy Keeper of the Records and two of the clerks of the department always attend', and arranged that Fraser be permitted to remain in office until 31 July. He was allowed the difference between the amount of his pension and the amount of his salary from 1 April to 31 July, at the rate of £200 per annum (which indicates that his pension was two-thirds of his salary of £600). [21]   Matthew Livingstone, Deputy Keeper of Sasines, was appointed to succeed Fraser on 23 July 1892, with the same salary of £600. [22]

# CHAPTER 3

## TRAVELS ON BUSINESS AND PLEASURE

Committed as he was, until his retirement in 1892 at the age of 76, to an office day (though admittedly not a very long one), at the Register House, Fraser had to fit in the bulk of his private work on peerage cases and family histories – not only research and writing in Edinburgh but also visiting muniment rooms and other places throughout the country – into time free from official duties. In May 1866, for example, he proposed to visit the burial place at Dalkeith on the forenoon of a Saturday which happened to be a 'free day' at the office;[1] it seems to have been the last Saturday in the month, the 26th, which was probably a holiday associated with the Queen's birthday and the opening of the General Assembly, which both fell on the 24th. In August 1877 he spent part of his 'official holiday' at Raehills (no doubt examining Johnstone papers which he would require for the Annandale Peerage Case and which would be useful for the *Annandale Book*, ultimately published in 1894) and at Drumlanrig (where he may have been tidying up some points for the *Buccleuch Book*, which was published in 1878, though by this stage he would be acceptable for a purely social visit to the Duke of Buccleuch's home).[2] On 24 August 1878 he wrote from Castle Grant (Grantown), when the publication of *The Chiefs of Grant* was five years off, that 'my holidays are now expiring and I must return home today'.[3]

It is impossible to construct anything like a complete itinerary, for the relevant information has to come mainly from extant correspondence and, while this is voluminous, preservation was a matter of chance and surviving details about Fraser's movements from this source are essentially fortuitous. The notebook 'diaries' which found their way to the National Library give us only a few patches of entries about journeys and visits.

The first of Fraser's known expeditions, which is also the one most fully documented, was a genuinely holiday or pleasure jaunt in 1840, when, aged 24 and still a clerk with an Edinburgh legal firm, he set off for London with Archibald Grant, another law clerk, with whom he shared lodgings. A day-by-day account, in the form of full notes of all items of expenditure, was printed in the Memoir prefixed to the *Fraser Papers*. It is worthy of reproduction here, not only for the light it throws on Fraser's attachment to 'the ancient Scottish virtue of thrift' but for the indications it gives of the great importance of steam navigation at a time when the railways were still in their early days and were much more expensive than waterborne travel. In that year the only railway to or from Edinburgh was that 'innocent railway' the Dalkeith line, opened in 1831 and using horse-drawn traction; the Glasgow line did not open until 1841, the Edinburgh, Leith and Granton not until 1842 and the Berwick line not until 1846.

EXTRACTS from the CASH BOOK of WILLIAM FRASER, Writer, Edinburgh, commencing 10th October 1839 and ending 31st December 1841

| Dates. 1840 | Particulars of Payments, etc. | Paid. £ s. d. | Received. £ s. d. |
|---|---|---|---|
| Aug.31 | By said Balance . . . | ... | 3 12 5 |
| Sept.4 | By Cash from Mr. Sands – | | |
| | For July writings. £6 14 3 | | |
| | " Augt. Do. . 18 8 6 | | |
| | | ... | 25 2 9 |
| | N.B.– Very hard labour this, independent of a good deal of writing in the Books. | | |
| " | Paid A.Grant for writing to me . | 0 1 6 | |
| " | Gratuity to Mrs Williamson's servant . . . . | 0 2 6 | |
| 5 | National Bank Dr. lodged. . . | 17 0 0 | |
| " | Paid Mrs. Wilson for washing . . | 0 0 6 | |
| " | Paid for purse and comb . . . | 0 0 11 | |
| " | Paid for postage stamps . . . | 0 1 0 | |
| " | Paid for maps . . . . | 0 0 9 | |
| | Took with me to England 1 £5 B. of England note No. 3749, signed 'T. Donald,' indorsed 'Marion Rutherfurd Philip' (something I can't make out), and signed by myself. Also 3 Sovs. and 5 ½ Do. gold and 11/4½ silver. | | |
| | To expenses of trip to England:– | | |
| Sept.5 | Paid porter to omnibus at the Tron Church with luggage for London £0 0 6 | | |

| | | | £ | s | d |
|---|---|---|---|---|---|
| Sept.5 | Paid omnibus to Leith | | £0 | 0 | 6 |
| 6 | Fare in the steamboat 'Pegasus' from Leith to Hull | | 0 | 7 | 6 |
| 6 | Ginger beer on board Do. for refreshment | | 0 | 0 | 4 |
| 7 | To the following at Hull in Simpson's,23 Humber St., opposite Victoria Rooms:- | | | | |

Paid supper, bed
and breakfast £0 3 6
Servant       0 0 2
           0 3 8

Paid for pies at
a confectioner's 0 0 7½
Paid for fruit 0 0 2½
Paid for
biscuits      0 0 1

           0 4 7

| 8 | Fare per 'Monarch' steamer to London (from Hull) | | 0 | 5 | 0 |
| | Coffee and biscuits on board Do. | | 0 | 0 | 4 |
| | Charity Do. | | 0 | 0 | 2 |
| | To my half of the following payments per A. G. for joint behoof, viz:- | | | | |
| 10 | Porter to W. Abbey | £0 0 2 | | | |
| " | Admission to Do. | 0 2 6 | | | |
| " | Guide Book of Do. | 0 2 0 | | | |
| " | Admission to H. of Commons | 0 1 0 | | | |
| " | Do. to Wr.Hall | 0 0 6 | | | |
| 11 | Cakes, &c | 0 0 3 | | | |
| " | Admission to London Monument | 0 1 0 | | | |
| " | Steam Boats from West - minster to pier near Monnᵗ. | 0 0 8 | | | |
| " | Cakes | 0 0 2 | | | |
| " | Apples | 0 0 1 | | | |

Sept.11 Boat to Tower 0 0 8
" Bread & Beer 0 0 4
" Admission to
Tower:-
Armoury . 1
Jewels . 3
0 4 0
" Small boat to
& from Tunnel 0 1 0
" Admission to
Tunnel, 1/-
each 0 2 0
" Steamer down
to Greenwich,
8d. each 0 1 4
" Music on board 0 0 1
" Pensioner at
Greenwich 0 0 1
" Admission to
Picture Hall
there,3d.each 0 0 6
" Steamer back 0 1 4
" Bread 0 0 2
" Convent (sic)Gar-
den Theatre 0 2 0
" Bill for Do. 0 0 1
" Recd. from
A.G. at the-
atre 0 1 0
12 Bread, &c.,
to Regent
Park 0 0 6
" P.P. stamps
for A.G. 0 1 4½
" Do. for W.F. 0 1 6
13 Fare to Win-
dsor on Gt.
Western Rail-
way,2/6 each 0 5 0
" Breakfast
there 0 2 6
" Admission to
State apart-
ments there 0 1 6
" Biscuits 4d.,
and Milk 4d. 0 0 8
14 Paid for soap 0 1 0
" Cap for W.F. 0 1 0
15 Grant's Jour-
nal for Do. 0 0 2

Sept.15 Music on board
        steamer   from
        Hampton Court  0 0 1
     16 Shoe laces for
        A.G.           0 0 1
      " Fruit for Do.  0 0 0½
        Catalogue of
        British Museum 0 0 6
                       £1 18 10
          -less-
        A.G.'s half              0 19 5
      " To my own half
        of the follow-
        ing payts.made
        by myself for
        joint behoof w^t
        A.G. -
     13 Fare per Great
        Western Rail-
        way from Wind-
        sor (2/6 ea.)  0 5 0
     14 Do. per South
        Western Do.
        to Hampton
        Court, 3 at 1/6
        (including Far-
        mer)           0 4 6
      " Foot tolls to
        Hampton Court  0 0 6
      " Guide book at
        Do.            0 0 6
      " Doorkeeper at
        Do.            0 0 6
      " Biscuits    at
        Richmond       0 0 6
      " Fares in ste-
        amer from Rich-
        mond to London
        3 @ 1/6        0 4 6
      " Music on board 0 0 1
     15 Paid for ink   0 0 0½
      " Grapes         0 0 8
      " Admission to
        St Paul's      0 1 4
      " Biscuits       0 0 6
     16 Bill at Hart's 3 1 6
      " Omnibus to R.-
        way, 6d.each,
        1/-, Hart's
        boots, 6d.     0 1 6

Sept.16 Fares per Lon-
        don & Bir. R.-
        way, 20/- each   2  0  0
    "   Dinner at Bir-
        mingham          0  2  0
    "   Biscuits Do.     0  0  6
    "   Fares to Liver-
        pool per Grand
        Junction Rail-
        way, 18/-        1 16  0
    "   Boy for carrying
        bag at L'pool    0  0  3
   17   Biscuits    on
        leaving Do.for
        Glasgow          0  0  4
    "   Lodgings    at
        L'pool, 5/-,&
        servants, 1/-    0  6  0
    "   Pears for Far-
        mer              0  0  6
    "   Refreshment      0  0  6
    "   Fares to Glas-
        gow p.'Actæon'   0 10  0
   18   Bed in Do. for
        W.F.             0  2  6
    "   Charity by Do.   0  0  6
    "   Music on board   0  0  1
    "   G. Bread         0  0  1
    "   Refreshment at
        Glasgow          0  1 10
    "   Do. on leaving
        Do.              0  0  4
    "   Fares in Canal
        boat home, 4/6
        ea.              0  9  0
                         £9 12  0½
        Deduct
        Items of above
        chargeable  to
        W.F. solely      0  5  5
                         £9  6  7½
        ½ to A.G.        4 13  3½
                         £4 13  3
        Add
        The above        0  5  5
        Add
   18   Additional
        items charge-
        able to W.F.,
        viz:-

```
Sept. 9 Dinner    in
        Coffee House 7d.
     "  Postages of
        letters    3d.
    11  Fruit      1d.
     "  Life of Xᵗ  1d.
                        0  1  0
           Total expenses      4 19 8
                                        6 18 0
    19  Dr.Ar.Grant:
        To half  of
        payments made
        by me as on
        preceding
        page                 4 13 3½
           Less
        ½ paid by you
        for me as  on
        page 32             0 19 5
             A. GRANT            3 13 10½
```

These mere 'bones' are brought to life in some candid passages in a journal. [4] Like most Scots on a first visit to London, Fraser thought the brick houses presented 'a poor and temporary appearance which contrasted with the more formidable and substantial stone structures of our Scottish metropolis'. His journey by train from London to Windsor was the first train journey he had made. At Windsor he attended the Sunday morning service in St George's Chapel, but the splendours of that building and its historical associations seem to have left him unmoved and his thoughts ran rather on a distaste for Anglican worship and on an almost contemptuous attitude to the Queen which would not have sat so well on the future K.C.B. 'To tell the honest truth, she did not appear to seem to me to be either a good looking, agreeable or intelligent woman. She has a very childish, puerile, insipid cast of countenance and her mouth in particular is of the fly-catching, continual gape, kind, and gives her rather a foolish look'. Prince Albert, by contrast, was 'a fine looking, fresh, blooming boy'. There were comments also on Victoria's mother, the Duchess of Kent, on Lord Melbourne, the Prime Minister, and on Lord John Russell, then Colonial Secretary.

In his early years Fraser probably had frequent recourse to sea-travel for journeys north, as well as south, from Edinburgh, for there was no train to Aberdeen until 1850, whereas steamers had been plying frequently and regularly since 1821, calling at several small ports on the way.[5] In October 1846 he certainly went north on the 500-ton paddle-steamer the *Duke of Richmond*, sailing from Newhaven and intending to land at Stonehaven, but she was 'swept past to Aberdeen by the violence of the storm' and he landed 'very sick and fatigued'.[6] Most of Fraser's subsequent travelling, even to nearby places like Dalkeith, was by train, and the extension of the railways must have greatly facilitated his work. Journeys to London became commonplace and seldom called for specific mention, but in 1879 he indicated that dangers lurked in the gloom of Victorian railway stations:[7]

> When I was seeing Mr Fletcher off to London by the late train on Saturday night, a tall figure, who had espied me by the lamp, came up to me, and I was relieved when he showered apologies instead of offering any injury.

The stranger was Sir Noel Paton.

For the period from May 1845 to November 1847 there has survived, to be reproduced in the *Memoir*, a 'Memorandum Book' which records Fraser's movements intermittently. From 3 to 20 May 1845 he was in Kincardineshire, and when his maternal grandmother, Jean Aitershank or Walker, died at her house near Cowie on the 14th in her 97th year Fraser was able to be at her funeral to Fetteresso churchyard on the 17th. He remarked that 'my father's father and mother and my mother's father and mother all died in the same house near Cowie'. When he left for Edinburgh he 'felt a good deal on parting with my friends, especially my uncle's wife'. Before the death occurred, Fraser was meeting professional men, especially ministers, who provided the most ready link between a man of Fraser's humble origins and those of high social status. Thus on 6 May he was the guest of the Rev. George Thomson at dinner at Fetteresso Manse, in the company of the Rev. William Mearns of Kinneff, John Watt, Thomson's assistant, and Professor Patrick Forbes 'of Old Aberdeen', who had become professor of Humanity and Chemistry at King's College in 1817. Two days later there was a similar party with the Rev. Alexander Silver at Dunnottar Manse, when 'Mr Smart and Mr Falconer, writers', were present. Next day he dined with Mr Smart, who had Mr Silver as another guest, and the following day he supped with Mr Smart. He renewed his acquaintance with his old employer and benefactor Mr Brand, for he dined with him and his wife on the 13th and breakfasted with them on the 19th, the day before he returned to Edinburgh. He attended Fetteresso Church on the 11th and a week later was at Dunnottar in the forenoon and Fetteresso in the afternoon. But there was business to be transacted too. When he dined at Dunottar Manse 'there was much talk' of the succession to Alexander Wood of Woodburnden, an estate two miles from Fordoun. On 14 May he 'went to Brechin in the morning and spent this and the following day in investigations about Mr Wood of Woodburnden's succession and had the good fortune to discover a common ancestor which establishes the claim of Mrs Farrell to about £60,000. A lucky hit for her. poor woman'. Mrs Farrell was the wife of John Farrell in Stonehaven. Evidently Fraser was also acting professionally for the minister of Fetteresso, for he records that on 7 June he received a presentation from the Home Office in favour of John Watt as Assistant and Successor in Fetteresso and sent it on to Writers in Stonehaven.

Back in Edinburgh Fraser took up business threads and there are indications of the range of his interests when he was still in his thirtieth year. There came a 'very excellent and satisfactory' letter from Patrick Chalmers of Auldbar, lately M.P. for Montrose Burghs, answering enquiries 'in regard to Dr Young, Dean of Winchester, and the Gib family etc.' John Young was a son of Peter Young, who had been James VI's tutor and who was buried in St Vigean's Church in Angus; no doubt all those 'enquiries' were genealogical. Fraser wrote a few days later to Mr Smart, the Writer in Stonehaven, 'with Memorandum of my searches in the Records here in support of Mrs Farrell's claim as heir of the late Mr Wood of Woodburnden'. On 10 September he 'attended the service of Mrs Farrell as heir of the late Mr Wood' and was present later in the day at what was no doubt a celebratory dinner 'in the Royal' – though the Service is dated 27 November in the Record of Services of Heirs. On 4 March 1846 Fraser notes that Mr Logan, the Teind Clerk, informed him 'that there are a great many old papers about Berwickshire families at Burnhall, the property of the late Mr Grant, also at Renton, the residence of Sir Samuel Stirling'; and on the same day he received letters from Colonel Spottiswoode about his pedigree and from Mr Smart about the Wood family. On 11 June 1845 Fraser had been in the Register House between 2 and 3 p.m. when Prince Henry of the Netherlands 'came in and saw the Register House, Records, etc. The Prince seems a plain intelligent young man'. On 15 November 1846 Fraser supped with Mr W.B.D. Turnbull, an advocate, and 'admired his splendid library'.

As a sequel to that foray into the Mearns in May 1845 an attempt was made to entice Fraser back into practice there. Silver, the minister of Dunnottar, acted – it seems a little odd – as intermediary: on 11 September Fraser had a letter from him asking 'if I would accept of a partner-ship with Mr Alexander Smart, Writer. Stonehaven. I

answered that I would, if the share was sufficiently liberal'. Nine days later came a letter from Smart himself,
which prompted Fraser to enquire what his business profits
had been for the last five years and what share Fraser
would have. Next month we learn: 'Mr Smart ultimately offered me a third part of his business, but after deducting
several of the best paying parts of it, which he reserved
to himself, I decidedly declined such a partial partnership
and so ended the affair'.

But with all the pressure of varied business there
was some time for relaxation. On the afternoon of Saturday, 7 June 1845, Fraser 'bathed at Caroline park – the
first time this season'. The place was a beach at Royston,
a little west of Granton; where, curiously enough, the
present writer bathed quite frequently in his schooldays.
From that rather humble and unexciting exercise Fraser
seems to rise from the almost ridiculous to the almost
sublime when he reveals sporting experience on the moors
which must have stood him in good stead when, in his
later and more distinguished days, he was several times
a guest at shooting parties with aristocratic hosts. He
records on 9 August 1845 that he took from the Rev. Dr
Laird of Portmoak the shootings (1200 acres) on his
estates of Colzium and Cairns in the parish of Midcalder
at a rent of £10 for the season. He was not sparing of
energy in his shooting. On 12 August he started at 3 a.m.
and from then until 7 p.m. walked 'full 50 miles',
bagging 8 brace of grouse, 'more than was ever known
to have been shot upon those moors in one day'. On 5
September he shot three hares, 3 brace of partridges, 2
brace of snipe and a brace of grouse. On the 16th he shot
at Craigiehall with 'Mr Sands and his son, but we were
not successful'. Next month he went to Stonehaven to his
uncle and aunt and his cousins at Alpity of Arbuthnott
and Knox of Benholm. He shot over Redmyre, Bridge of
Leppie and Whiteriggs and also at Tullo of Garvock ('Mr
Scott's') and Middleton, where he killed two partridges
and a hare at a single shot. At Redmyre, Whiteriggs etc.
he killed 12 hares and 3 partridges. 'I have killed in
all these excursions, never having a whole day from the
wetness of the weather, about 60 head of hares and partridges'. He dined with Mr Alexander Burnett and breakfasted with Mr Brand and returned to Edinburgh on 25
October. He noted that his dog Frisk, which he had had
since 1837, disappeared on 21 March 1846 but came back
in April, only to be sent away to Mr Dunlop at Cumber-
nauld House.

After that sequence of entries in the *Memoir*, covering
1845-6, we have only stray references for the years 1847
to 1851. In 1847 he was at 'Kinnaird and other places in

Forfarshire' and in 1848 at Lord Galloway's in 'the west of Scotland' – presumably Galloway House at Garlieston in Wigtownshire – and then in East Lothian. [8] In October 1849 he examined the burgh records at Irvine and in January 1850 (not an ideal month for travelling) he made something of an assault on the south-west: Drumlanrig, St Mary's Isle, Galloway House, Kenmure Castle and other places. [9] In November 1851 he was at the Duke of Montrose's residence at 'Buchanan House', where a disastrous fire had destroyed the old mansion in January 1850. [10] Then follows a period of ten years for which we have no information.

For the early 1860s we have fuller particulars again. In September 1861 he was in Renfrewshire, [11] and in October there begins a series of diary entries [12] which carry on to 1867. Surely at this time on leave from the office, he was first in the west – Rossdhu on 22 October and Glenfruin on the 24th – and then, after a weekend at home when he was present at the Sacrament in St Cuthbert's on the 27th, in and around Fife: Wemyss Castle, Melville House and Cullairnie on the 28th, Kinfauns and St Andrews on the 30th. In 1862 he was away from Edinburgh earlier in the season, at Murthly Castle in Perthshire on 9 July; and in August he was back in the west: Helensburgh on the 24th and Dumfin (near Bannachra, Luss), next day. In September 1863 a large number of engagements were compressed into four days, spent mainly in Angus. He seems to have prefixed to his account of his actual movements a note of the places he meant to visit: Leuchars, Inverkeilor, Ethie, Balnamoon, Farnell and Kinnaird. On the 7th he was with Lord Northesk at Ethie, with Mr Ashley at Inverkeilor Manse, with Mr John Carnegie at a place unnamed and at the manse of a minister identifiable as George Walker, minister of Kinnell. Next day he was with Mr Carnegy Arbuthnott at Balnamoon and on 9 September he was at Kinnaird Castle, residence of the Earl of Southesk. We know from another source that he was at Saltoun six times between December 1862 and June 1864.

One of the many visits to Lord Elphinstone's home at Carberry took place in 1864, then in 1865 he was for some time in 'Athole', at Dunkeld (possibly calling at the Duke of Atholl's residence) on 15 July and on dates unspecified at Murthly and Grandtully (both residences of the same Stewart family), partly to make notes on documents for the Grandtully Book, after which he was in the west again, at the Colquhoun seat of Rossdhu. In April 1866 he was in Perthshire once more, at Drummond Castle, then owned by the Willoughby de Eresby family who became Earls of Ancaster, and in December he visited Alloa, where he no doubt conferred with the Earl of Kellie on his claim

to the earldom of Mar. [13]   In June 1867 he seems to have
broken new ground by visiting 'Colquhouns in Glasgow'.
The remaining known visits in this decade were in February 1869 to Saltoun Hall once more and in the following
month to Johnstonburn (also in East Lothian, the home of
Archibald Broun). [14]

Throughout the 1870s the information is on the whole
thinner. On 25 September 1872 he mentioned that he had been
at The Hirsell, the seat of the Earl of Home in Berwickshire, [15]  and in the same year he revisited Carberry (as
he did again in 1883). On 14 June 1873 he was at Tulli-
allan, a residence which had been built by George Keith
Elphinstone, Viscount Keith, and had passed to his
daughter, who by this time was Lady Osborne. [16]  Fraser's
movements were, of course, dictated largely by the needs
of the family histories and other projects, including
peerage cases, but it was also true that he established
with his clients a relationship which meant that they
made him welcome as their guest: thus in 1873 the Marquis
of Tweeddale invited him to Yester 'on a friendly visit'.  [17]
(A few years later, we learn, Fraser advised Tweeddale
on what title to choose should he be offered a United King-
dom peerage).[18] Fraser visited Inveraray in September 1873
and probably at other times, for when he wrote about the
fire there in 1877 his words suggest that he had recent
knowledge of the place.[19]   In August 1877 he was again
at Raehills with the Johnstones, combining business with
pleasure, for he joined in grouse-shooting with his
hosts. [20]  On the same trip to the south-west he was at
Drumlanrig again as well as at Lockerbie. The last year
for which we have much information is 1878, when he
travelled widely. He was at the Lake of Menteith on 10
August and left an entertaining account of the company
there: 'The weather here has been very fine, and I have
improved upon the change. This lake has been well
guarded by Admirals of H.M. Navy. Admiral Erskine has
a beautiful residence on its banks and he has staying
with him another Admiral, Lord Edward Russell, who
claims to be an uncle of Lady Dalkeith. Yesterday when
at Buchanan the first person that Her Grace introduced
me to was another Admiral – Sir Reginald Macdonald, "Chief
of Clanranald" as he has engrossed on his card which he
presented to me. It is not always that fresh water lakes
attract so many salts.'[21]   Fraser was at Castle Grant on
24 August 1878 and in 'the Reay country' of the far north
on 10 October. He was at Hamilton Palace in July and
August 1879, Donibristle in February 1880 and Kilconquhar
in September 1880. [22]

For many years, if not all through, the early habit
of noting all expenditure continued, for the surviving

notebooks record every trifling item. He lunched for nine-
pence at Glasgow on 22 October 1861. But the notebooks
show also how wide-ranging his curiosity was as he moved
about the country. He took notes, apparently just as
casual opportunity arose, on buildings, families and
portraits, adjoining properties and their owners, tombs,
inscriptions, armorial bearings, family Bibles and of
course documents, and he sometimes incorporated with such
jottings notes from the *New Statistical Account*. He anticipat-
ed some of the work done in more recent years by
interviewing aged inhabitants, though he did not have the
advantage of a tape-recorder. Thus at Helensburgh in
August 1862 he noted the recollections of a man of 91.
Near Luss next day he noted traditional history from a
man of 88 and learned that Lady Helen, wife of Sir James
Colquhoun of Rossdhu, gauged the eggs of 'kain fowls',
rendered by tenants among their dues, by using a ring:
if they were small enough to drop through they were
rejected. Fraser sought information from aged informants
once more, this time in Angus, in September 1863. His
many visits to manses were not always mere social
occasions, for when he visited the minister of Inverkeilor
in 1873 he consulted presbytery records.

CHAPTER 4

PEERAGE CASES

Fraser's interests were so dominated by peerage cases and
the preparation of family histories, which went on concurrently through most of his working life, that one does
not readily consider which of the two came first and
whether one led to the other. It seems that his genealogical and antiquarian interests, added to his professional
qualifications, caused his engagement in peerage cases
before he planned any family histories. It may be that
he owed his introduction to both peerage work and family
histories to Cosmo Innes, whose clerk he was for a time
in the 1840s: Innes had acted in the Forbes case (1830–
32) and was crown agent in the Stirling case (1839), when
the claimant was tried for forgery, and then it was no
accident that Fraser's first family book was *The Stirlings
of Keir* (1858), in which Innes, as well as John Dundas,
the Keir agent, collaborated.

Although Fraser may have been engaged as a consultant at some previous point, the first case in which
he gave evidence seems to have been Marchmont. That
earldom had been dormant since the death of the 3rd Earl
in 1794. It was claimed by Alexander Home, a descendant
of a brother of Patrick, first of Polwarth, and after
Alexander's death in 1823 by his son Francis. In Fraser's
time a case had been going on since 1838 and he came
in as a witness at the final hearing in 1843,[1] to authent-
icate productions from the Register of the Great Seal, the
Justiciary Court Records and the charter chests of Billie
(Berwickshire) and Argaty, The claim did not succeed,
owing to the failure to extinguish intermediate lines.
Fraser was engaged in the Glencairn case in 1847, when
he corresponded with Sir Thomas Montgomery Cunninghame
of Corsehill, Bart., Colonel Cunningham of Coldstream and
Cunningham of Craigends, all of whom were claimants, and
it was possibly in this connection that he obtained notes
of Cunningham entries in the Matriculation Rolls of
Glasgow University.[2] No claim succeeded, and the earldom
remained dormant, as it had been since 1796. Fraser
played a bigger role in Southesk, from 1847:[3] he appeared

in the House of Lords in 1848 and was the main witness in 1854–5, when his evidence ran to 200 pages and the claim to the forfeited title was successful.

As peerage cases were apt to go on for years, Fraser was sometimes engaged in two or three concurrently. Thus his employment in Southesk coincided with the Herries case (1849–51), in which he had been engaged since July 1848. [4] His designation as a witness in 1849 was 'Writer in Edinburgh', and he was said to have been much engaged of late years in inquiries concerned with peerage cases. He was acting on behalf of Mr Maxwell of Carruchan, the petitioner against the claim of William Constable–Maxwell to a title forfeited in 1716, and he produced extracts from the Acta Dominorum Concilii et Sessionis, Liber Responsionum, Register of Deeds and Register of the Privy Council. In 1851, now designated S.S.C., Fraser swore to extracts from the Acts and Decreets, Register of the Privy Council, Register of the Great Seal and that less obvious source the Accounts of the Sub–Collectors of Thirds of Benefices, besides documents from the charter room at Kenmure. The case did not end until 1858, when the decision went against Fraser's client. In the same years when he was occupied with Southesk and Herries, Fraser seems to have agreed to act as consultant in the Kenmure case (1848), [5] over a peerage which had become dormant in 1847 after being restored in 1824. He was also employed by a claimant to the Hyndford title, which had been dormant since 1817: [6] Sir John Anstruther was heir general of the Carmichael family who had held the title, but the last holder had a nephew, Archibald Nisbet of Carfin.

Fraser was by no means the only expert available in a period when peerage cases were uncommonly numerous. Alexander Deuchar, a professional genealogist, gave evidence in the Airth case in 1839; George Robertson, Deputy Keeper of the Records, acted (as Fraser did) in the Herries case; and George B. Robertson, next Deputy Keeper of the Records, acted in Kilwinning (1860–7), Breadalbane (1867–72) and Borthwick (1869). J.C. Brodie acted in Lovat (1855–7), designated 'member of the firm of Gibson Craig, Dalziel and Brodie'; in Kilwinning (1860–7), now designated a Writer to the Signet; and in Balfour of Burleigh (1862) and Belhaven (1874) with the designation Principal Keeper of the Register of Sasines. W.L. Christie, 'conveyancing clerk to Dundas and Wilson,' acted in Kilwinning; and the Rev. J. Anderson, who was 'frequently employed in transcribing and translating ancient records deposited in the General Register House' acted in Dysart (1880). Other cases in which Fraser does not seem to have been involved were Crawford (1845), Dundonald (1861), Kinloss (1867) and Lauderdale (1885).

After his earlier essays in Marchmont, Southesk, Herries and others, Fraser was heavily committed in three major cases – Montrose (1850–5), Mar (1868–73) and Lindsay (1877). The Montrose case was one of uncommon historical interest, for the Earl of Crawford and Balcarres was claiming the Dukedom of Montrose which had been created for the Earl of Crawford by James III in 1487 – the first dukedom in Scotland to be conferred on anyone other than a son or brother of a reigning sovereign and apparently a personal honour. to be held for life but not to be transmitted by descent. The proceedings are recorded in three volumes of MS. and two of print, one of them extending to over 600 pages and the other to 300 pages. Fraser, who told Crawford firmly in 1850 that his claim was not justified,[7] collected evidence on behalf of the Duke of Montrose, holder of the hereditary title created for James Graham, Earl of Montrose, in 1707. He made a crushing comment on one document in 1853: 'On examining the Patent with reference to the Montrose case, I find that it has neither the great seal nor even a tag for it appended. The name of the Chancellor is erased.... These defects would be fatal'. [8] By the time Fraser appeared as a witness he was Assistant Keeper of the Register of Sasines and he gave nearly 200 pages of evidence on productions of extracts from public records and on documents from the Glamis, Craigends, Montrose, Drummond and Buchanan charter chests.

The Mar case was of course one of the most celebrated in Scottish peerage law. Fraser had been engaged not later than 1866 by Walter Coningsby Erskine, Earl of Kellie, [9] who claimed an earldom previously held by his cousin, John Francis Miller, Earl of Mar and Kellie, who died in 1866, and he prepared a Memorial for the claimant in 1867. Fraser's view was that there had been two earldoms of Mar, an older one which had lapsed and a second, created by Queen Mary for Lord Erskine in 1565. Once the case was over, he explained in a letter to John C. Brodie: 'When I went to Alloa in December 1866, to inspect the Mar muniments, I told the late Lord Kellie that I had made a preliminary investigation into the Mar Peerage through documents in my own possession. and that I had come to the very decided opinion that the original earldom of Mar had been extinct for upwards of four centuries and that the peerage which now existed was a new creation by Queen Mary. Lord Kellie had never heard of the New Creation, and he was startled with my announcement of it. I asked if he would be satisfied with the more modern dignity. He replied, with emphasis, "If you can get me that Mar title in any form, I will spend my last shilling for it". From the first I have never

faltered in my faith that the existing Mar peerage was
the one created by Queen Mary.' [10] Fraser first supported
his submission in 1868 and ultimately gave some 250 pages
of evidence, on productions from the Register of the Great
Seal, the Register of Sasines, the Retours and the Testaments, documents from the 'Exchequer Treasury of the
Receipt' and writs from the Douglas, Wigtown, Forbes,
Torphichen and Buccleuch charter chests. G.B. Robertson,
Deputy Keeper of the Records, was also involved in this
case. The original claimant, the 12th Earl of Kellie, died
in 1872, and it was his son, Walter Henry, 13th Earl,
whose right to the earldom of Mar was recognised in 1875.
A telegram sent to Edinburgh on 25 February announced
'Judgement given unanimously declaring Lord Kellie Earl
of Mar'. [11] Fraser was proud to be awarded a 'large share
of victory' and mentioned that he had received 'a shoal
of letters from Lord and Lady Mar and many of their
friends, all expressing great satisfaction with the judg-
ment'. [12] However, controversy was not stilled, and
rumbled on for another twenty years. John Francis Goodeve
Erskine, nephew of the Earl of Mar who died in 1866,
succeeded his uncle (through a female) as Earl of Mar
of the earlier creation and he continued to challenge Lord
Kellie's title to an earldom of Mar. In 1892 he entered
protests in the House of Lords against Mar and Kellie,
to the indignation of the latter, who declared that
'Goodeve [Mar] and Galloway made fools of themselves'.
Fraser was again brought in and had to lay aside other
work to deal with this matter. Mar's protest was unanimously rejected. [13] One of the problems in the Mar case
had involved some missing charters. In 1870 Cosmo Innes
confirmed a statement by Fraser that '"the Mar charters"
as they are called' had been in the Register House in
Thomas Thomson's time, when Innes consulted them and
printed two items from them in the *Acts of the Parliaments*
vol. i. Besides, as Fraser reported in 1873, 'while the
chests were in the Register House a person still living
informed me that he very frequently obtained from Mr
Thomas Thomson and Mr Alexander MacDonald, who had
both access to the Mar Chests, numbers of charters on loan
without any receipt'. The family had recalled the material
and although 'repeated requests were made for documents
said to be in the Mar Charter Chest, it has been made
clear that they are not there and have never been seen
since'. In 1870 in the House of Lords 'Lord Kellie and I
[Fraser] were examined and re-examined about the missing
charters and we came out of it I think quite triumphantly.
We succeeded in rejecting a good deal of the enemy's
evidence'. [14]
    The Lindsay case (1877–8) followed hard on Mar. This

earldom had been held for a century and a half by the
Earl of Crawford, then in 1808 it reverted to the heirs
male of the Lords Lindsay of Byres, but it was only in
the 1870s that the right was recognised. Fraser had the
co-operation of the Reverend Walter MacLeod, whom he
often employed as a searcher and transcriber. Fraser's
own evidence in the case ran to more than 300 pages,
relating to records (Register of the Great Seal, Parliament-
ary Papers, Retours, Testaments, Sheriff Court Book of Fife
and a Register of Baptisms) and to the charter chests of
the Earl of Hopetoun, the Earl of Glasgow and Sir John
Trotter Bethune (who was the petitioner). Bethune
succeeded in his claim and Fraser was hailed as 'William
the Conqueror'. [15]

Concurrently with the Lindsay case there was the
Annandale case. The male succession to the marquisate
of Annandale had failed in 1792 and it had been claimed
by John James Hope Johnstone as early as 1820; a grand-
son of the same name was the claimant in the proceedings
of 1877–81, in the course of which Fraser gave evidence,
producing documents from the Register House and from the
charters of Annandale, Buccleuch, Winton (Earl of Eglinton), Leven and Melville, Hamilton and Douglas. Walter
MacLeod and the Rev. J. Anderson also gave evidence.
This claim failed. The argument turned partly on the
validity of the resignation of the dignities (with a view
to a new infeftment) during the Protectorate. In 1877
Fraser brought to the notice of the Lord Advocate the
analogy between the resignation of the Buccleuch dignities
in Exchequer in 1650 and the resignation of the Annandale
dignities, also in Exchequer, in 1657, and the Advocate
agreed that this had an important bearing on the Annandale case. [16] However, the Lords would not acknowledge
the validity of a resignation made in the hands of Oliver
Cromwell as Protector, and Fraser commented on 3 June
1879: 'at Holyrood last night His Grace the Lord High
Commissioner taxed me with attempting to make Cromwell
one of the kings of England'.[17] (By a curious coincidence,
the compiler of this account of Fraser's work was engaged
as a consultant in a renewed assault on this peerage.)

Fraser's 'evidence' in all those cases consisted for
the most part in simply authenticating documents, testify-
ing to their location and to the accuracy of the transcripts. The transcribing would not usually have been his
own work, but he must have collated the printed texts
with the original MSS, so that even at the lowest the
extensive evidence given in peerage cases involved a very
great deal of time in the preparation of submissions.

Not many of the peerage cases are directly related
to the family histories which Fraser produced – Southesk,

Montrose (Lennox) and Johnstone are instances – but every peerage case gave him the opportunity to lay his hands on the contents of charter–rooms, some of which were used for the histories of other families. Besides, he made notes on the titles of various families which might or might not contribute to either a peerage case or a family history: Eglinton and Winton and Menteith and Airth are examples,[18] and we shall see later how much time he spent on arranging the Argyll muniments.

# CHAPTER 5

## THE FAMILY HISTORIES

In the preface to Fraser's first family book, *The Stirlings of Keir and their Family Papers* (which was produced at the expense of Stirling of Keir) the hope was expressed that 'the example thus set – probably the first work of the kind executed by a Scotch proprietor at his own charge – may yet be generally followed by the owners of other ancient charter-chests'. This was prophetic, for it set the pattern for another twenty-three works, extending to forty-nine volumes:

The Montgomeries, Earls of Eglinton, 2 vols., 1859
The Maxwells of Pollok, 2 vols., 1863
The Maxwell, Herries and Nithsdale Muniments, 1865
The Pollok-Maxwell Baronetcy, 1866
History of the Carnegies, Earls of Southesk, 2 vols., 1867
The Red Book of Grandtully, 2 vols., 1868
The Chiefs of Colquhoun and their Country, 2 vols., 1869
The Book of Caerlaverock, 2 vols., 1873
The Cartulary of Colquhoun, 1873
The Lennox, 2 vols., 1874
The Cartulary of Pollok-Maxwell, 1875
The Earls of Cromartie, 2 vols., 1876
The Scotts of Buccleuch, 2 vols., 1878
The Frasers of Phillorth, 3 vols., 1879
The Red Book of Menteith, 2 vols., 1880
The Chiefs of Grant, 3 vols., 1883
The Douglas Book, 4 vols., 1885
The Family of Wemyss, 3 vols., 1888
The Earls of Haddington, 2 vols., 1889
The Melvilles, Earls of Melville, and the Leslies, Earls of Leven, 3 vols., 1890
The Sutherland Book, 3 vols., 1892
The Earls of Annandale, 2 vols., 1894
Lords Elphinstone, Balmerino and Coupar, 2 vols., 1897

While Fraser visited muniment rooms assiduously, the amount of time he could spend in them was limited, partly because of his office commitments and partly because of seasonal constraints imposed by the length of the day and the temperature. On 16 April 1860 he remarked that 'the weather now admits of my working in charter rooms for several hours at a time'. [1] The bulk of his transcribing and note-taking, whether for peerage cases, his books or the Historical MSS Commission, must have been done in Edinburgh, to which great quantities of material were transmitted. He explained in 1859: 'When a charter chest is too far from Edinburgh to admit of my visiting it easily, the whole of the papers are transferred to Edinburgh. But when a charter chest is within easy reach. I go out and make a selection of the contents. This saves removing many papers which are not needed'. [2] Even when this limitation is taken into account, however, the bulk of papers removed to Edinburgh was very considerable. The Duke of Buccleuch's home at Dalkeith, for example, was easy enough of access, yet several letters refer to the movement of documents between that home and Edinburgh and when the *Buccleuch Book* was completed, in 1879, there are particulars of boxes returned to the Duke's charter room and a request for a cart to convey ten or eleven boxes. [3] As long as Fraser was on the Register House staff, material sent to town for him to work on may have been temporarily deposited in the security shared by the public records, but it may well be that most of it went for shorter or longer periods to the Castle Street house, where what Fraser called his 'charter room' [4] was pre- sumably situated. It is not to be assumed that all Fraser's work, even on the national archives, was done within the walls of the Register House, for attitudes then were far less strict than they later became, and Dr Maitland Thomson, I have been told, used to trundle the unwieldy volumes of the Great Seal Register to his home when he was editing that record.

Fraser could not have achieved a fraction of his immense labours in correspondence, transcribing, collating, proof-reading and overseeing publication without a great deal of paid assistance. An astonishingly large proportion of his letters, especially in his early years, even if they are long and deal with matters of detail, are in his own clear and consistent hand, but many are not holograph and he clearly employed amanuenses. Transcription and collation were of necessity delegated to men skilled in the palaeography and diplomatic of Scottish documents and records. One of those whom Fraser employed was the Reverend Henry Paton, who attained some success not only as a genealogical searcher but also as as editor of a considerable number of volumes, including the *Acta Dominorum Concilii 1496-1501*, the *Register of the Privy Council*, 3rd series, vols. ix-xiv, and that remarkable compilation the eight volumes of *Records of Clan Campbell*, and who was in addition joint author, with J.W. Buchan, of a three-volume *History of Peeblesshire*. Another expert whom Fraser employed was the Reverend Walter MacLeod, who, like Paton, was a Secession minister but of a branch in competition with Paton's and who edited part of the *Protocol Book of John Foular*, the *Journal of Erskine of Carnock* and a selection from *The Family Papers of Dundas of Dundas*. Walter MacLeod's son John joined his father in his later years. Other assistants of Fraser, designated only by their initials in notes about collation of documents, are not so easily identified, but at the time of his death Sir William had four 'clerks' - the Rev. William Scott, Mr Gibb, Mr MacLeod [that is, presumably James, brother of John], and Mr Buchanan. [5]

There is a receipt to Fraser in 1878 by Walter MacLeod for payment in consideration of 'collating proofs of documents in the Buccleuch Book with records in the Register House with J. Anderson'. The latter was presumably the Rev. J. Anderson whose work in transcription led to his employment in the Dysart peerage case and who edited the *Laing Charters*. The payment was '3 hours each 9s. and 2 hours each 6s.', which means that each was paid 1s. 6d. an hour. [6] Another statement indicated that 'clerks' were paid 1s. per page for transcribing and 12s. a day for collating. [7] The latter payment, given an eight-hour day, again suggests 1s. 6d. an hour. Oral tradition (as recounted to me by the late Dr C.T. McInnes) has it that Fraser paid only 6d. an hour, but clearly this did not apply to at any rate his more skilled employees. At the same time, if Fraser is open to the charge of being parsimonious as an employer, this reflected the engrained habits of economy of a man who, as already indicated, noted every trifling expense on his travels and who habitually used scraps of paper, often paper already written on one side, very much as his contemporary the Rev. Hew Scott, industrious compiler of the *Fasti Ecclesiae Scoticanae*, made his notes on old envelopes. A memorandum by Fraser on the titles of honour of the Duke of Montrose was written on the reverse of sheets of proofs of a printed inventory. [8]

Although we know something of Fraser's visits to muniment rooms and other repositories, about his correspondence with his clients and about his employment of transcribers, it is difficult to form a clear picture of the many stages which intervened before the production of one of the histories. There is only a glimpse here and there

of the painstaking work which went into the preparation
of the text and the correction of proofs. Two file jackets
in the Lothian MSS contain transcripts of documents relating to the Kerrs and to Jedburgh Abbey, made in 1885–
6 and marked to show how they had been collated and
revised: 'collated by W[illiam] F[raser]', 'collated by Mr
Anderson and Mr Gibb', 'hand–collated A.G., collated
W$^r$.S., A.G.', 'doubly collated' and finally 'revised' by
Fraser in 1894.[9]

It is not always possible even to establish the length
of time for which Fraser was engaged on the preparation
of a particular history, but some of the histories represented work carried on intermittently during two decades or
more. The four volumes of *The Douglas Book* did not appear
until 1885, but references to work which presumably con-
tributed to it extend back more than a quarter of a
century. In 1857 Fraser had correspondence with Lord Home
about the claim of Lord Douglas to the earldom of
Angus:[10] he was working on 'Douglas Papers' in
1860;[11] in 1864 he was examining title deeds of Glenbervie
in the period when the property belonged to Douglases;[12] he
was at The Hirsel in 1872, examining some of the papers
of Lord Home, who could claim to be the senior representative of the Douglas family;[13] in 1879 he had arranged
'to get into the Duke of Hamilton's charter room at
Hamilton before finishing the Douglas Book';[14] and in 1880–
1 he had correspondence with Lord Home, the Earl of
Crawford and the Librarian of the Advocates' Library
about a missing volume of Douglas–Angus correspondence,
monuments in St Bride's Church and other matters.[15] Work
on *Buccleuch*, which was published in 1878, went on for
twenty years, perhaps longer. Fraser had corresponded
with the Duke of Buccleuch from 1855;[16] in 1859 he mentioned that the Buccleuch history would require the use of
papers from Wemyss Castle, Leslie House, Polwarth, Scott
of Ancrum and Yester;[17] in 1861 he reported to the Duke
that the examination of the charter room at Dalkeith was
'nearly finished', which must mean the preliminary survey
to determine what would have to go to Edinburgh;[18] boxes
of papers were sent from Dalkeith to Edinburgh in 1861,
1862, 1866 and 1873;[19] and as late as 1877 Fraser spent
two days in the charter room at Drumlanrig.[20] The first
copy of the book was despatched on 24 December 1878.[21]

Most of the information about the collection of material
for the family histories relates, it will be observed, to
private muniments. As to research in the public records,
hardly a trace remains, and far too little to indicate how
Fraser and his employees found their way about the
largely unindexed volumes. Like other searchers, however,
Fraser evidently had some indexes of his own, for there

is an item titled 'Kerrs and Jedburgh Abbey, notes from my own index of the Register of the Privy Seal', ranging in dates from 1582 to 1629. [22]

While some indications can be found of the length of time during which a history was in preparation, we know much less about how long volumes were in the press. Yet it is evident that more than one family history could sometimes be with the printers simultaneously. *Buccleuch* certainly overlapped with *Frasers*. The latter was being produced on a commission from Lord Saltoun, [23] and Fraser explained to the Duke of Buccleuch in May 1877: 'Owing to the continued indisposition of Lord Saltoun a large quantity of type is locked up in the Fraser Book, and as the type in both books is similar it would be a great favour if your Grace could return the Memoir, soon, as the printer will require part of the type for the next Memoir, of the 1st Earl of Buccleuch'. [24] The problem of type being 'locked up' may well have occurred more than once.

Fraser seems to have had a persistent interest in illustrative material, which became in practice very important in his volumes, and seized opportunities to obtain copies of portraits in particular. Thus in 1872 he obtained a copy of the Southesk portrait of the Great Marquis of Montrose; [25] in 1875 he sent Lord Lothian copies of portraits of the Earl of Ancram 'from Lord Saltoun's original' and of Cecil Drury from lord Polwarth's miniature; [26] and in 1877 he added an engraved portrait of Buccleuch to those he already had of Southesk and other celebrities. [27] In the production of his volume, he paid attention to the quality of the illustrations as well as to their subject-matter.

Like other authors, Fraser occasionally had the mortifying experience of discovering some flaw after the twelfth hour, and after the first copies of *Buccleuch* had been despatched he gave the Duke an assurance that 'a trifling error in the pedigree' would be corrected in copies not yet issued, presumably by amendment in manuscript. [28] He had been luckier over an error in a supposed marriage of a daughter (actually a sister) of Murdoch, Duke of Albany, to a Campbell of Lochawe, for this was discovered in time and Fraser took the opportunity to deliver some remarks about accuracy: 'It shows how much care is required to attain absolute accuracy in such works. From the nature of them, they never can be wholly free from a certain amount of error. But I am thankful that I have been wonderfully lucky, with so many chances of error, to keep them within a minimum.' [29] Although he put his own accuracy down to an element of luck, he was not so ready to see the errors of others as a result of bad luck: when in 1873 he sent the Duke of Montrose a note by Alexander Sinclare on the Montrose peerages, he observed that Sinclare 'has a great deal of genealogical information, but as he is not a professional man, but an amateur, he sometimes falls into mistakes'. [30] An error of a different kind, which does seem to have caused Fraser some sense of embarrassment, was his mislaying of a copy of the 'Confession of Faith' (that is, the National Covenant) which had been lent to him by Lord Lothian and which Fraser had caused to be repaired in 1875 at a cost to Lothian of two guineas. Apparently in 1879 Fraser could not find it and hoped that Lothian had it. However, Lothian, after making a search, asked, 'Would you have another look for it?' and Fraser admitted to finding it in his 'charter room', adding: 'You may believe in my own confession of deep regret and contrition for causing you so much trouble. Although no excuse, I may say that I think this is the first great sin of the kind I have committed. From my earliest years I have been always finding and not losing papers, and I hope my faculties are not failing'. Lothian very civilly congratulated Fraser on 'how securely you keep all the documents in your charge'. [31]

At the last, or almost the last, stage of production, Fraser gave his personal attention to the binding. For example, when *Buccleuch* was ready for issue, in December 1878, he noted: 'I have restricted him [the binder] with the morocco backs to the copies for the family only'.[32]

Finally came distribution, when Fraser no doubt found it highly agreeable to play the munificent patron to the noble friends who, under another guise, were his paymasters, and to act as a generous donor even up to the level of royalty. It might have been unreasonable for a man so fully occupied as Fraser was to have calculated that judicious distribution of copies of his works might bring him fresh commissions, but it is a fact that when Tweeddale wrote to acknowledge a copy of *Buccleuch* in 1879, he explained: 'I shall be strongly tempted to ask you to undertake a similar work illustrative of the Hays. I am afraid the expenses of such an undertaking are very large. But we might talk over this some day at Yester, where I hope to spend the autumn this year.'[33]

It may be doubted whether clients whose hearts had grown sick by the repeatedly deferred hopes of their own family histories were mollified by receiving gifts of others, but receive them they did. Buccleuch, whose own volumes did not appear until 1878 although Fraser had been working for him since the late 50s, received *Pollok* in 1861 (at the desire of Sir John Maxwell of Pollok), *Grandtully* in 1869, *Colquhoun* in 1870 and *Lennox* in 1874. [34] Lothian, for whom Fraser worked intermittently from 1860, without in the end writing a book for him at all, was similarly

favoured, with *Pollok* in 1871, *Cambuskenneth* in 1872, *Frasers* in 1875, 'Athole' [surely *Grandtully*] in 1879, *Wemyss* in 1888 and *Melvilles* in 1891, and in 1879 Fraser was trying to find a copy of *Stirling* for him.[35] Lothian seems to have taken immense pride in his acquisitions of Fraser's volumes, and his appreciation must have been highly gratifying to the author. Already in 1883 he congratulated Fraser on 'the splendid addition to the long and ever increasing series of portraits of your children [i.e., books]' and added, 'this last effort [*Grant*] which has resulted in triplets, certainly beats any of the others.'[36] When *Wemyss* arrived in 1888, he wrote, 'I look forward to the placing this latest-born by the side of his numerous brothers in "the Fraser nursery" at Newbattle'.[37] In 1894, on the delivery of *Annandale*, Lothian acknowledged 'the beautiful books', which were to be placed at Newbattle in 'the Fraser Nursery, to the glories of which they added a new effulgence. I counted my – or rather your – children and they number 47 [volumes]....
I feel proud to own them and to know that they occupy *the* place of honour in a library which is not without other values'.[38] Only six months later there was a further acknowledgment: 'A 1000 thanks for your note and for sending the books', part of 'your ever-increasing family'.[39] It is not clear to which this last reference relates, for no volume came out in 1895 and *Annandale* had been acknowledged in 1894: the possibility cannot be discounted that Fraser had unearthed spare copies of some earlier volumes, but it may be that he had sent Lothian copies of some of his H.M.C. Reports, as he did to Seafield, who placed them in 'The Fraser Compartment' of his library.[40]

Royalty, apparently, was first reached through intermediaries: the Duke and Duchess of Buccleuch took a copy of their own family book to Queen Victoria in 1879.[41] But in 1891 Fraser arranged for *Haddington* and *Melville* to be taken to the Queen by Lord Haddington,[42] and in 1894 *Sutherland* was received by the Queen and the Prince of Wales.[43] Other notables, below royal rank, were not forgotten, for W.E. Gladstone got a copy of *Wemyss* in 1890 and Lord Rosebery one of *Elphinstone*. A volume in the National Library contains a whole series of acknowledgments, including the following: from Cosmo Innes (*Stirlings*), Queen Victoria (*Grandtully*), John Denison, Speaker of the House Commons (*Colquhoun*), Duke of Argyll (*Grants*), James Grant, author of many historical novels and of *Old and New Edinburgh* (*Grants*), Lord Lovat (*Grants*), Lord Advocate J.B. Balfour (*Menteith* and*Annandale*), Lord Salisbury ('four valuable volumes' in 1885, presumably *Douglas*), the Prince of Wales ('the work', in 1891, presumably *Melvilles*), W.E.Gladstone ('valuable works', 1893), Lord Haddington

(*Sutherland*), Sir John Stirling Maxwell (*Sutherland*). Lord Rosebery (*Annandale*) and Lord Wemyss (*Annandale*).[44] Another volume in the National Library contains acknowledgments from Gladstone, Salisbury, the Duke of Argyll, the Marquis of Dufferin and Ava and others.[45]

In the case of *Buccleuch*, out of 150 copies to be printed, Fraser proposed the presentation of about 130 – over 80 to individuals, over 30 to libraries and institutions, a dozen to Fraser for making over to 'professional gentlemen by whom he has been assisted', reviewers etc. In due course acknowledgments were received from, *inter alios*, Mar and Kellie, Seafield, Saltoun, Minto, Bute, Mark Napier, Thomas Gladstone of Fasque, Montrose, Argyll, Eglinton, Atholl, Polwarth, Cawdor, Dalhousie, Wemyss, Rothes, Rosslyn, Salisbury, the Bibliothèque Nationale in Paris, the Signet Library, the College of Arms and the Library of the Lyon Office. Glasgow University Library, the British Museum and the Dundee Public Library received copies, but the Mitchell Library, though it applied, was turned down.[46] (This library, however, received volumes from the Trustees after Fraser's death.) Lord Herries approved of the presentation of sixteen copies of *Caerlaverock*.[47]

Complications could arise subsequently about the fate of volumes which had been presented. Copies of *Cromartie* and *Grant* were sent in 1877 and 1883 to Sir Bernard Burke, Ulster King of Arms, for his office, with a clear statement that there were no extra copies for his private library. The two works were acknowledged by Ulster on 8 August 1877 and 1 November 1883 respectively; in the second acknowledgment he stated that *The Chiefs of Grant* 'occupies a prominent place in Ulster's Library'. After Burke's death in 1892 the catalogue of his library, to be sold by his executors on 28 March 1893, included the Fraser volumes, and Vicars, Burke's successor as Ulster, admitted on 24 November 1894 that both MSS. and printed books had been carried off from the official library by Burke's family. Fraser was not alone in his indignation. Lord Seafield, in letters to him dated 4 and 11 January 1895, observed 'that MSS and printed books belonging to the government could be abstracted by anyone and publicly sold is monstrous... Nothing could be more clear than that you presented the books to the Dublin Ulster Library and that Sir Bernard Burke accepted them for that library'. It made matters worse, as Fraser complained to W.A. Lindsay at the College of Arms on 20 December 1894, that the volumes had been sold at 'such "enormous prices" that even the government did not attempt their purchase'. From the College of Arms there came first (11 January 1895) an enquiry 'Are you *sure* the presentations were not to Sir Bernard by name?' and then (16 January) an admission that books belonging to Ulster's Library had been sold as Sir Bernard's own. It appears, however, that all the stir did not result in the recovery of the volumes. [48]

While in the case of those Ulster volumes it added to Fraser's irritation that the prices had been so high, in general he derived a good deal of satisfaction and even pride from the increasing value of his books and sometimes regretted that he had not retained more copies for himself. In 1871, when he sent Lord Lothian the copy of *Pollok* which Sir William Stirling Maxwell had authorised him to present, he remarked: 'If no other it will have this advantage that its great size will help to fill up some vacant space. There is perhaps also a little pecuniary advantage which has been tested by the sale of two copies of deceased presentees for about seventeen pounds each copy'. [49] And to Buccleuch he wrote on 23 March 1878: 'at a late sale 18 of my books were put up in one lot' at £180 and were soon up to £254. A bookseller said that if the lot had been complete to include all the Family Books they would have brought upwards of £300 and that if I had 20 copies of the set they would be worth £6000. But I have not that and nothing like it'. [50]

A later section will show that Fraser's work did not go without criticism, but there was no disputing that the volumes were treasured. A review in *The Edinburgh Review*. July 1879, ran: 'Few are the copies in existence, and favoured are the lovers of rare books who can boast of this addition to their libraries. for no care and no expense have been spared in the production of these ducal volumes [*Buccleuch*], in which, as has been said, "a rivulet of text meanders through a meadow of margin".[51]

It would appear that Fraser (or perhaps his patrons) sometimes presented copies of his books to the Register House, for in a letter to Pitt Dundas in 1869 he rather characteristically suggested that future official reports might mention gifts of rare books, especially books containing charters both printed and lithographed.[52]

# CHAPTER 6

## THE HISTORICAL MANUSCRIPTS COMMISSION

When the Historical Manuscripts Commission was set up in 1869 to report on MSS in the hands of private individuals and corporate bodies, it recruited men who were already expert in historical documents and records and who were employed by the Commission on a part-time basis. The first Scot so appointed was John Stuart (1813-77), an Aberdeen advocate who did notable work as a founder of the Spalding Club, Secretary of the Society of Antiquaries of Scotland and editor of many volumes of historical source material. Stuart had been one of the official searchers of records at the Register House in 1853. This was the year after Fraser became Assistant Keeper of the Register of Sasines, but Stuart was Fraser's senior by three years in age and his output of published work – mainly in the shape of his incredible labours for the Spalding Club – rivalled Fraser's in quantity and represented a wider range of source material. It would not have been surprising if he was thought the better scholar. Stuart was to become Principal Keeper of the Register of Deeds in 1873, whereas Fraser (who was passed over in 1857 for the Principal Keepership of the Sasines) did not become Deputy Keeper of the Records until 1880. [1]

Stuart's appointment with the H.M.C. was made with the approval of the Lord Clerk Register and on the understanding that he was not to use official time for the Commission's work. This arrangement was generally believed to work well and without prejudice to the work of the office, though John C. Brodie had some reservations on the subject, and it was almost at once decided to recruit Fraser on the same conditions. On 15 June 1870 the Master of the Rolls wrote to the Lord Clerk Register suggesting that Fraser should be appointed. and the Lord Clerk Register approved, observing that Stuart's work for the Commission had 'occasioned no detriment to the public service in the Searching Department'.[2]   On 19 October following. with the agreement of the Treasury, the Clerk Register and the Master of the Rolls Fraser was appointed an 'Inspector of Historical MSS for Scotland', with the same remuneration as Dr Stuart.[3] As the office hours were then 10–4 from Monday to Friday and 10–2 on Saturdays, there was plenty of time for unofficial work, but it was hard to see how much could be done by way of visiting repositories except during periods of annual leave. However, the amount of HMC work which could be done was limited by finance, for while payment was at the rate of £2.2s. per diem, the total payment in a year was not to exceed £63, which meant a total of thirty days' work. This arrangement continued year by year.[4]

The earliest reports on Scottish collections, in the *First Report* of the Commission in 1870, were all done by Stuart, but Fraser, immediately on his appointment, threw himself into work for which he was eminently fitted and which he must have found highly congenial. He began with a long description of the muniments of the Duke of Montrose at Buchanan in the *Second Report* (1871), which he introduced in those words: 'A few days after receiving my formal appointment, on 1st November 1870, as an Inspector for Scotland, I had an opportunity of bringing the objects of the Commission to the notice of the Duke of Montrose.... Upwards of twenty years ago I made a careful examination of all the documents deposited in the Muniment Room at Buchanan in reference to the old Dukedom of Montrose, which was then claimed by the late Earl of Crawford and Balcarres; and having afterwards frequently examined the papers for other purposes, I have been long familiar with their contents. The Original Papers being chiefly in my own custody, I am enabled to report on them in greater detail than I could have done had they all been at Buchanan'.[5]

Fraser did nothing else in that *Second Report*. For the third (1872) he made a second report on Montrose, along with Lennox, Menteith and some others. At this stage he mentioned briefly that 'chiefly in the course of my short official vacations, inspections were made ' of the muniments of Buccleuch at Drumlanrig, Roxburghe at Floors, Blantyre at Lennoxlove, Fletcher at Saltoun and others. As Stuart's health was failing, and he died in 1877, the ball was at Fraser's foot, and there followed a number of major reports which continued almost as long as he lived: Arbuthnott and the Earl of Glasgow in the *Eighth Report* (1881); Eglinton and Winton, Sir John Stirling Maxwell and Stirling–Home–Drummond–Moray (1883); Duke of Hamilton (1887); Earl of Home (1888); Duke of Atholl (1890); and Buccleuch I (1895, published 1897).

Fraser was all along adept at killing two birds with one stone. It has been mentioned how work on one book complemented work on other family histories and how work on a peerage case could contribute to the preparation of another. This technique applied with special force to the work of the Historical MSS Commission, because many of Fraser's reports were on muniments which he had already examined for peerage purposes and for family books. In reporting for the Commission he was presumably under no particular constraint as to his choice of material and was free to make his own selection. It is quite likely that his reports may have consisted very largely of material which he had already noted for one or other of his own manifold purposes and it might not be going too far to say that he was open to the charge of receiving a double payment for covering the same ground twice over. Possibly this lay behind the curiously phrased accusation which Mark Napier was said to have made in 1873. that Fraser had made a calendar of the Montrose muniments at the public expense: [6] to do so was of course perfectly proper in working for the HMC, but what Fraser may have done was to hand over to the Commission a calendar already made for other purposes. But a certain uneasiness in Fraser's mind or conscience may have been the occasion of a letter he wrote to Lord Lothian in September 1882. At the time, Lothian had been keeper of the privy seal since 1874, but he did not become Secretary for Scotland until 1886, and Fraser can only have had an eye to influence which Lord Lothian could exert behind the scenes. At any rate, he lent Lothian his reports on Elphinstone, Traquair, The Binns and Monymusk, as specimens of the work done for the Commission. He explained that as he held another office he was not allowed to do more than thirty days' work in the year for the Commission, or at least was not paid for doing more (at 2 guineas a day), but that in practice he sometimes went beyond the officially designated limits of time. without additional payment, rather than suspend operations at an inconvenient point.[7]

In addition to the Family Histories and the Reports issued by the Commission, Fraser was the author of *A Genealogical Table of Lt.-General Sir T.M. Brisbane* and *Genealogical Tables of the Families of Brisbane of Bishopton and Brisbane, Macdougall of Makerstoun and Hay of Alderstoun, from Family Title-deeds*, both published in 1840. He edited the *Liber S. Marie de Dryburgh* for the Bannatyne Club in 1847 and the *Registrum Monasterii S. Marie de Cambuskenneth* for the Grampian Club in 1872.

# CHAPTER 7

## 'DRIVING FOUR IN HAND'

In a letter to be quoted below, Fraser complained that he
was 'literally obliged to drive four in hand'. He was
referring only to the many volumes of his family histories
which were in progress, but his entire activities extended
not only to the four headings of official business, peerage
cases, family books and the HMC, but also to a number of
varied ploys which, as anyone in a similar position
knows, can cumulatively take up a great deal of time.

So late at least as 1870, busy as he was with official
work and the preparation of material for family histories
and peerage cases, he could still make time for private
investigations, at any rate for personal friends like
William A. Loch of the Drylaw family. On 3 October 1870
he wrote to Loch: 'One of my clerks, who is an amateur
photographer and has his holidays at present, went to
Cramond and photographed the inscription stone in your
Family Burial Place. I send enclosed a print of his
photograph.' Loch's grandfather. it appears, had been in
treaty for the estate of Drylaw, but could not reach agreement on the value of Craigleith Quarry, and Fraser
commented: 'For his own sake I wish that he had seen
better through the stones, as ... the revenue from the
quarry alone was £4000 a year'. Fraser also offered
information about a portrait of Queen Mary and promised
a photograph of Drylaw. 'But it may be a little time before
I can overtake it, as I have been much occupied with
visitations since I saw you. In one of these I encountered
Lord Burleigh, whom we pommelled successfully for Lord
Eglinton in his claim for Kilwinning, and this morning I
left at Melville a very agreeable cousin of yours, Mrs
Ramsay Campbell, who is on a visit to Lady Elizabeth
Cartwright'. Three days later Fraser wrote again to Loch,
intimating that he made additions to Loch's family tree,
from 'Registers of Births etc.' of Edinburgh and Cramond,
and suggesting that the genealogy might be extended by
the Records of Edinburgh Town Council, Testaments and the
title–deeds of Drylaw, but adding, 'You may not care to
incur the expense of these searches at present. as there
is no peerage or property dependent upon them'.[1]

Anyone in Fraser's position must have been pestered, as those on whom part of his mantle has in any sense fallen still are, by genealogical enquirers, but the evidence for this lies mainly in his official correspondence as Deputy Keeper of the Records. He knew exactly what answers to give, and did not suffer fools gladly. In 1883, in reply to a Mr Forbes in Cape Breton, Fraser wrote that there was a *History of Clan Mackay* by John Mackay and that he should apply to Mr Paterson, Bookseller, 67 Princes Street, Edinburgh; [2] and a few days later he referred another genealogical enquirer to the Lyon Court. [3] At the beginning of 1888 one Percy Easton asked Fraser for his pedigree. Fraser replied – astonishingly for a man so fully occupied, and occupied with remunerative work – that he was willing to make a search in his private capacity but added: 'I am unable to furnish you with the probable cost of any such inquiries, as it is impossible to foresee what repositories will require to be searched'. [4] A classic answer, which may have been used many times. It may be significant of Fraser's whole approach to those who sought information that the sharpest tone I have found in his correspondence is not in a letter to a private enquirer but in one in 1888 to the Crown Agent, who wanted lists of burghs of barony and regality from the 'Record of the Great Seal, in your custody as Keeper of the Records'. Fraser told him to go and look at the printed volumes of that record as far as they went and then suggested that someone should be employed to continue the search in the MS volumes at a rate of 3s. per hour or 18s. a day, and wound up: 'The person who had asked for the list of burghs to be supplied does not appear to have any adequate idea of the time and labour involved. [5]

It is not surprising that Fraser frequently complained of pressure of work. As early as 1859, the year after the appearance of his first family history, *The Stirlings of Keir*, and the year in which the second, *Eglinton*, was published, he remarked that 'family histories are now very popular.... I have undertaken as many as may occupy my lifetime.' [6] This was prophetic, for he was in fact fully launched on the labours which extended over the next four decades, until his death in 1898. He almost certainly took on far too much – perhaps more than was fair to his clients as well as to his own peace of mind – but he seems to have been unable to resist the importunities which crowded on him as his reputation grew and it became such a fashion for a family of note to have its history compiled by Fraser that his volumes became something like status symbols. To judge from two letters to Lord Lothian, Fraser's thoughts on the subject of his heavy commitments found expression in almost stereotyped phraseology. Thus in 1874, when Lothian had evidently commissioned him to compile a Cartulary of the Abbey of Jedburgh, he wrote: [7]

> I am most gratified by your kind commission to undertake a work which from my experience has become very familiar and congenial to me and I hope to be spared to finish it to your satisfaction. With so many other works on my hands I cannot promise rapid execution.

And four years later, after Lothian had commissioned a family history, Fraser wrote: [8]

> Owing to the number of other commissions which I have already in hand of similar works for other families and the many claims upon my time for other business, I cannot promise very rapid execution.... I hope I may be spared to complete it.

And he added, 'When Dr John Brown was told that I had undertaken to write a history of the Argyll family, he said to me, "We must just pray for long life to you"'[9]. In 1883 he professed to be almost overwhelmed: 'The Douglas Book will occupy a considerable time, and three other books are pressing as well as it, that I am literally obliged to drive four in hand, so that even with the Douglas Book finished the claims upon my time for other books would be as incessant as ever'.[10]

Dr Brown's prayer that Fraser might have a long life was granted, for the genealogist lived to be eighty-two. While he had the means to ensure his comfort and his protection against damage to his health, he must have had considerable reserves of strength to stand up to the labours which required not only unremitting toil at his desk (or desks) in Edinburgh but also lengthy travels throughout the country and spells of toil in charter rooms with their hazards of cold and dust. In 1861 he complained of 'feeling colded' after an expedition to Renfrewshire.[11] His not infrequent references to his health suggest that he took good care of himself, and an attack of pleurisy early in 1869 (from which he convalesced at Saltoun Hall) may have given him some fear of colds. [12] Writing from London early in May 1870 he remarked that the weather had been very cold and that Sir W.S. Maxwell and he had had to add 'our thicker coats' on their way south. [13] In December 1874 he mentioned that he had 'a cold upon me'[14] and in December 1877 he explained in characteristic terms how the cold weather had affected his movements on an Edinburgh Sunday: 'After breakfast yesterday Lady Elphinstone arranged with me to go to church with her. But I was afterwards induced by the cold weather and Lord Southesk and Lord Elphinstone to stay with them'.[15] In May 1878,

when he was nursing toothache, he was offered a trip to
Inchkeith: 'I am rather glad your letter did not arrive in
time to be a temptation to me to accompany you, as I
doubt if I could have stood the sea breeze with my toothache'.[16] A reference in 1883 to 'the present state of my
health' [17] may indicate some passing indisposition or undue
concern, for he was to live for another fifteen years. His
travels only once involved him in an accident. and then
the cause was not the pursuit of charters: 'The fall referred to in Mr Fleming's letter occurred to me last month
when at Glenferness. The family had never seen the old
castle of Lochendorb, and we had a large expedition to it.
A canny pony was assigned to me, but they omitted to
warn me that it shied at an umbrella. As soon as my
umbrella went up, the pony threw me down on my head.
I was stunned for a time. But I was able to make out the
journey'.[18]

It was obvious that to write the history of a family
it was not sufficient to ransack that family's archives,
for much relating to it could be found in the archives of
other families. Thus already in 1859 Fraser found that for
the Buccleuch family there was relevant material at
Wemyss Castle, Yester and the papers of Scott of Ancrum
and Lord Polwarth; a search for missing Douglas and
Angus correspondence led him into communication with the
Earl of Crawford and the Earl of Home; and work on
*Buccleuch* also involved correspondence with Lord Dundonald about a letter from a Duchess of Buccleuch to an
ancestor of Dundonald. [19] On the other hand, the collection
at Dalkeith, used primarily for Buccleuch, yielded material
for other families and charters relating to the Mar peerage. [20] To that extent, having many irons in the fire could
actually be advantageous. This Fraser realised as early
as 1849, when he was asked to act in the Kenmure Case
and remarked: 'Instead of retarding, one peerage case
helps forward another, inasmuch as more extensive
investigations are necessary and what serves for one case
frequently turns up something favourable for others.'[21] In
the same year John Gibson, W.S., told Lord Home that the
writer and 'Mr Fraser' had encountered a patent of Baron
Home of Berwick while investigating documents in the
Herries Case. [22] Another example of a combination of quite
discrete interests came in 1862, when Fraser. writing to
the Earl of Home on the subject of the sale of Paisley by
the Earl of Angus to the second Earl of Abercorn, took the
opportunity to return a pedigree of the Rev. William Home.[23]
When examining charter chests either for his own ploys or
for the HMC, Fraser's eye could be caught by items of
significance for Scottish record studies generally: in 1861
he mentioned that in the Dalkeith charter room he had

found Melrose charters as well as letters of Adam Smith and a memorial of Simon, Lord Lovat; in 1874 he sent the Duke of Buccleuch a translation of a charter of Alexander II; and some years later he told Lord Lothian that he had found a privy seal of David II in 'a Highland charter chest'. [24]

Moreover, despite the ever-growing pressure of his major occupations, Fraser could always find time to follow up bypaths which caught his imagination and to correct errors or misrepresentations. Thus in 1855 he noted a discrepancy in accounts of the movements of the Duke of York (later James VII) in July 1684: the Register of the Privy Council gave him as sitting on the 22nd and the 24th, but the Duke wrote from Tonbridge on the 22nd and from Windsor on the 25th. [25] Four years later Fraser was concerned with the fascinating question of the right of the Duke of Abercorn (as heir male of the 2nd Earl of Arran) to the French duchy of Châtelherault which had been conferred on that earl, as distinct from the duchy created by Napoleon III for the Duke of Hamilton, who was heir of the 2nd Earl of Arran through a female. [26] More than once, in the course of his researches in the Buccleuch archives, Fraser referred to the question of the supposed marriage of Charles II to Lucy Walker, mother of the Duke of Monmouth and ancestress of the Duke of Buccleuch· the impression one forms is that Fraser was inclined to believe that there was something in the story, if only to the extent that there was a marriage by habit and repute. [27] Fraser mentioned in 1878 that the latest legend he had disposed of was that of 'Muckle-moo'd Meg'; [28] and as late as 1892 he was occupied with the problem of Margaret Bruce, second daughter of King Robert I, whose history, he remarked, 'has cost me as much labour as the Mar heiresses'. [29]

The firmness and even acerbity which he sometimes showed in dealing with the tiresome and the importunate went hand in hand with a certain amount of humour, an occasional light touch and some banter between Fraser and his clients, especially Lord Lothian. After *Buccleuch* had been issued (at the end of 1878), Fraser wrote that someone had been afraid of opening 'the marvellous book ... on account of the risk. The innocent effigy of the wizard, Michael Scott, which is on a very diminished scale, must I think be the real cause of terror, as the opening of his book in Melrose Abbey was also attended with alarm'. [30] The depiction of Michael Scott, which is indeed on a very diminished scale, is on a sheet between pages xxxiv and xxxv of *Buccleuch* vol. i, and the allusion was to incidents in *The Lay of the Last Minstrel*, but Sir Walter's epithets for Michael's book were 'mighty', 'mystic' and

'wondrous', not 'marvellous'. Witticisms, it must be said,
sometimes occur in the context of Fraser's conceit. In 1883
he mentioned that he had written to Sir Herbert Maxwell
'protesting against his being called Lord Protector by
*The Scotsman*, as Lord Lothian calls me Lord Protector of
the Records and Peers of Scotland and there cannot be two
Lord Protectors'.[31] When in 1875 Fraser sent Lord Lothian
a request for payment of £20 for copies of two portraits,
2 guineas due for repairing a copy of the 'Confession of
Faith' and £7.17.6 for a lithograph of the foundation
charter of Newbattle, he asked also for £50 for 'a fourth
tradesman. I mean myself', for 'the expense which I have
incurred for the proposed Cartulary of Jedburgh'.[32] In 1882
he had occasion to explain that 'Bog o' Gight' was Gordon
Castle and was familiarly called 'The Bog'; Charles II,
he mentioned, landed nearby in 1650 and had to be carried
ashore on the back of a fisherman (who as a reward got
a house rent-free in perpetuity). Fraser went on to relate
that the king dated a letter from 'The Bog' and added:
'When I showed it to Prince Leopold at Taymouth, he
screamed with laughter'.[33] Lothian frequently spoke of
Fraser's 'family' of books and to 'twins' and 'triplets',
but Fraser, writing to Buccleuch in 1878, said, 'Lord
Saltoun is to have a third volume for the Frasers. but I
have always maintained the orthodox twins. although they
may be rather corpulent'.[34] When Fraser was knighted,
Lothian took up what had evidently been a witticism of
Fraser: 'How glad I am that in your own amusing phrase
a Doctor has been slaughtered and a new and doughty
knight has taken his place. It is most fitting that the
name which has been the foremost in crystallising all that
is most noble and memorable in the rolls of the old
Scottish nobility should itself have a place in the Roll of
Honour'.[35] The Earl of Rosebery wrote at one point to
Fraser, 'Where are you? Pruning and watering some
obscure genealogical tree'.[36]

The man's industry seems to have become almost
legendary in his own lifetime. for he reported with amusement in 1894 that a reviewer of *Grant* in 'a north country
newspaper ... gravely stated the rumour' that the author
had dealt with 'many tons' of paper at Castle Grant.[37]

# CHAPTER 8

## UNFINISHED PROJECTS

Working as he did under such pressure, and undertaking so much, but at the same time clearly reluctant to refuse invitations made to him, Fraser inevitably embarked on, or contemplated, projects which were never completed. Curiously enough, the man who suffered most from Fraser's inability to match promise with performance was his generous client the 9th Marquis of Lothian, on whose remarkable patience Fraser was tempted to presume. Of all the projects which never attained fulfilment the one which seems to have dragged on longest was a proposed Cartulary of Jedburgh Abbey. At some date not later than 1860 Fraser had been commissioned by the 8th Marquis of Lothian to prepare such a Cartulary[1] and it appears that work on it went on intermittently, if only in a somewhat desultory manner, for the rest of Fraser's life. At the end of 1870, when the 9th Marquis had just succeeded to the title, Fraser sent him a facsimile of a charter granted by Malcolm IV to Jedburgh which he had discovered 'some years ago' and he remarked that 'your late lamented brother many years ago wrote me to make a cartulary of Jedburgh and I made some progress in collecting charters etc., of which this is a specimen'.[2] Nearly two years later, in another letter to Lord Lothian, Fraser mentioned that he had found a bundle of Jedburgh charters among Lord Home's papers at The Hirsel and added that he was 'always keeping a collection of Jedburgh charters in view'.[3] There was further correspondence in October 1874: Lothian at that point renewed the commission to compile a cartulary[4] and Fraser replied, in a letter already quoted, that he could not 'promise rapid execution'.[5] Fraser had received a box of MSS from the Lothian archives at New-battle in 1860 and he received another in 1878.[6] In 1875, when he had been 'picking up a number of documents connected with Jedburgh', he asked for £50 for 'the expense which I have incurred for the proposed Cartulary of Jedburgh',[7] and 1879 he received a cheque for £79. 19s. 6d. from Lothian.[8] The work was at one stage – or perhaps at more than one stage – at such an advanced stage that lithographs of charters were prepared: there is a note of six Glamis charters which were lithographed for the Jedburgh Cartulary at an unspecified date,[9] and in 1887 there is a discharge by lithographers of an account for Jedburgh charters. [10] There are references, too, to charters of the priory of Restenneth (a dependency of Jedburgh) [11] and to two file jackets containing documents relating to the Kerrs and to Jedburgh, some of them marked 'collated by W.F.' in 1885 and 1887. [12] The commission to Fraser (which, it was noted, contained 'no restriction of time'), was renewed again so late as 1891, and he was still collecting material so late as 1893.[13]

A second project for which the unfortunate Marquis of Lothian was enthusiastic but in which Fraser seems to have achieved even less than he did for Jedburgh was a History of the Ker family. Agreement that such a book should be done had been reached in 1861,[14] but as late as 11 March 1878 Lothian asked Fraser 'to authorise me formally on paper to begin ... to build up the material for a family book for me. The Kers of Ferniehirst and vol. II the Kerrs of Newbattle. I shall consider that a feather is wanting in the family cap if you do not take its history into your hands'.[15] Fraser was now (13 March 1878) understood to be formally commissioned to write a history of Lothian's 'historic house'. [16] Whether Fraser did much systematic work may be doubted, but he did note relevant items of information as he came across them. For example, in 1877 there is a note on the acquisition of the lordship and barony of Jedburgh by the Ker family in excambion for The Hirsel, [17] and in October 1874 Fraser and Lothian were in correspondence about a peerage supposed to have been conferred on Mark Ker, Commendator of Newbattle, in 1580: Lothian, who took an active interest, reported that he had found a monogram MKN 1580 with a baron's coronet.[18] Equally, when Fraser heard of relevant documents available for sale, he would acquire them either for himself or his client. For instance, in February 1870 he negotiated for the purchase of a letter of Robert Ker, Earl of Somerset, James VI's favourite, and beat the seller down from 4 guineas to 3; the purchase was made for Lord Schomberg Ker, who shortly afterwards succeeded his brother as 9th Marquis, and Fraser remarked: 'I have carefully avoided the names of yourself or your brother in connection with my inquiries – otherwise the price might be doubled'. [19] Then in 1876 he bought two Newbattle charters from a London bookseller, one for £2. 10s. and the other for £1. 1s. 6d. [20]

As both the Jedburgh Cartulary and the Ker History were still in the category of current work when Fraser died, his executors had to arrange for the return to Lord

Lothian of a considerable quantity of papers which had been in Fraser's hands for a long period. [21]

There was yet another project in which Lord Lothian had an interest, and that was a History of the Borders. Fraser wrote to him in June 1872: 'Your lordship has frequently alluded to a history of the Borders. In three books which I have now in hand on Border families, I am getting up a good deal of general history which has never before been noticed about the Debateable Land and other subjects'. [22] The three books he had in mind were *Buccleuch* (Scott), *Douglas* and the never-to-be-completed *Kerr*. But he had already written on the Maxwells in *Caerlaverock* (1873) and he was yet to produce the Johnstone book of *Annandale*, so there was certainly a great deal of Border history ready to hand. The Duke of Buccleuch took a lively interest in a possible Border History.

One more proposed publication, on which Fraser seems to have done as much work as he did on any, was a History of the Argyll Family, a project which may have been so massive as to daunt even him and which occasioned Dr John Brown's remark, 'We must just pray for long life to you'. [23] It is in connection with the Argyll family Muniments that we have the most copious evidence of Fraser's methods of working and of assessing his fees. There are accounts extant at Inveraray [24] showing that Fraser was engaged in work for the Duke from 1862 to 1897, with a gap in the record only from 1874 to 1879, and as some of those accounts are in draft form they provide a clear insight into Fraser's day-to-day activities. The account for 1862-6 'for the arrangement of the Argyll Family Muniments' consists of expenses in 'repairing charter chests before removing them to Castle Street', carriage of boxes from the Register House to Castle Street, other repairs to boxes, the making of casts of seals and visiting Saltoun six times 'selecting the correspondence of the Argyll family in the charter room there', and fees totalling £34. 10s. for the time of clerks 'for several months' in assisting in the arrangement of documents and 'getting them cured of damp', plus £25 for Fraser's own time in 'examining and arranging the charters and miscellaneous papers contained in 20 large chests.... also correspondence, about thirty letters'. The entire account ran to £66. 14s. 3d. Between 1866 and 1868 Fraser was engaged not only in examining papers but also in proving Argyll's right to the volume of royal letters already referred to: this he did by examining the business papers of 'the late Messrs Ferrier, W.S.', the annual reports of Thomas Thomson, Deputy Clerk Register, which had been 'founded on by Mr Dundas', and other material, and preparing a

letter to the Lord Clerk Register showing Argyll's right to
the volume. There were some minor expenses for boxes and
for a frame for a charter by Cardinal Beaton, coming all
told to £59. 18s. 9d. The accounts for the five years that
follow are the most illuminating, though why such heavily
corrected and amended drafts should ever have gone into
a client's hands is a mystery. There are thirteen pages
listing items, many of them crossed out because taken
account of in a sum mentioned later: writing letters
(usually at a charge of a penny for the postage, or a
halfpenny for a postcard), meetings with His Grace,
making transcripts and translations, making and repairing
boxes and documents, searching in the Mar and Castle
Menzies charter chests for Argyll documents, as well as
the major task of arranging muniments. In August 1869 we
learn that when the Duchess was entrusted with 'the box
containing the Argyll royal letters, the Cardinal Beton
charter and the Grantully Book, to be taken to Inveraray', a clerk was paid for an hour and a half's time in
'packing said box'. The total in those 1869–74 accounts
amounted to £32 4s 5d., which covered, besides the minor
items, over 200 hours of labour by Fraser and his clerks,
ten days work being at one point assessed at only five
guineas. A letter of 20 October 1877 recalls the restoration
of the royal letters and contains interesting comments on
Inveraray: [25]

> Some years ago I recovered for the Duke of Argyll,
> from the Register House, a valuable volume of royal
> letters of the Argyll family. I often urged the Duke
> of Argyll to get a special fire–proof safe for the
> volume. But the Duke thought it ran no more risk
> than the castle of Inveraray itself. I dreaded that it
> had been burned, as the volume was generally kept
> near where the fire raged. But I have a letter from
> Lord Lorne mentioning that it is quite safe, and he
> thinks that he has become as much engrossed in such
> things as myself, as he thought of them first before
> he thought of going for the ladies. He got the volume
> safely through the burning hall before he got Lady
> Caroline Charteris through it.... The Inveraray fire
> will be a good wind for the fire–proof safe.

The next extant account, covering 1879–92 and marked
'superseded by later account to December 1897', is a tidy
effort. It details all the work done – largely searching for
Argyll material in the charter chests of Hamilton, Donibristle, Sutherland, Mar, Breadalbane, Atholl, Douglas,
Dunstaffnage, the Scottish and English public records and
Edinburgh University Library, transcribing and collating
and also providing His Grace with historical information
about early conveyancing by charter, ancient leases and

certain events and relationships. The cost, however, is covered in summary fashion – 'occupied in all during the period of this account, thirteen years or 210 days [that is, for the clerks and Fraser together]: 52½ days at £2. 2s. per day [for Fraser] and clerks' time 158 days at 21s. per day £166. 10s. 5½d.' With some fees for transcriptions, labour amounted to £329. 10s. 5½d., and expenses for postages, tradesmen, travelling etc. made it up to a total of £340. 11s. 10½d. However, a different account purports to cover from October 1879 to 1894, as follows:-

| | | | | £ | s | d |
|---|---|---|---|---|---|---|
| Time | Sir William Fraser | 55 days @ £1.1s. | | £57 | 15s | 0d |
| Time | Clerks | 154 days @ £1 | | 154 | 0 | 0 |
| Letters 177 | | | @ 3/4 | 29 | 10 | |
| Sheets* 165 | | | @ 2/ | 16 | 10 | |
| Postages etc. say | | | | 1 | 10 | |
| Paid to woodengraver | | | | | 5 | |
| Paid to lithographers | | | | 15 | 17 | 6 |
| Paid to joiner | | | | 2 | 3 | 3 |
| Paid to ironmonger | | | | 1 | | 6 |
| | | | | £277 | 12s | 3d |

Those skilled in arithmetic may make sense of it all, as presumably the client or his agents did at the time. All the accounts are neatly docketed, 'Paid' with the dates.

One can only speculate as to whether there was any link between Fraser's labours on Argyll and the pipedream of an Argyll Book, on one side, and Henry Paton's eight volumes on *The Clan Campbell*, which appeared between 1913 and 1922, on the other. Paton's work, however, was based on official records rather than on private archives.

There were occasions when Fraser did a great deal of work on family muniments without necessarily a plan for a family history. Thus between 1862 and 1865 (when the stream of family books had little more than started) he arranged the Castlemilk and Torrance muniments, which were bound in fifteen large volumes.[26] A little later he was occupied with the Panmure papers.[27] The Hamilton of Dalyell Papers in Motherwell Public Library, recently surveyed for the National Register of Archives (Scotland), contain letters of Fraser concerning proposed work on this family's muniments and referring to his other publications, 1866-78.

* Presumably transcripts and translations, assessed at so much a sheet of writing.

Along with the unfinished projects reference may be made to an undertaking which Fraser did not originate and which did not remain unfinished though it might have been better had it done so. This was the 'Return of the Members of Parliament for Scotland', compiled in 1878. In 1887 Fraser wrote to the Secretary of the Public Record Office on the subject of the errors and deficiences in this work and went on: 'The late Lord Clerk Register [Gibson Craig], under whose direction the Return was compiled, thought that the labour bestowed upon it is lost time. He made a representation to Mr W.H. Smith, who was then at the Treasury, to stop the preparation. But Mr Smith said that it had proceeded too far and could not be stopped. The mover for the Return originally was my namesake Sir William Fraser, Bart., then M.P.'[28]

# CHAPTER 9

## THE RECKONING AND THE REWARDS

The family histories brought congratulations to Fraser and gratification to those who received copies as gifts, but the gratification of those who commissioned them was sometimes tempered by the fact that the production of the volumes had to be paid for. It seems that Fraser normally met all costs as they arose and then recovered his outlays after he submitted to his clients the receipts for payments in respect of searches, transcripts, collating, photography and lithography, as well as printing and binding. The costs of printing and binding were then such a mere fraction of what they are now that they accounted for what seems almost a ludicrously small proportion of the total expenses. For the two sumptuous volumes of *Buccleuch* the bill of the printers, Constables, was £744. 3. 6., including £195. 3. 6 for 'proofs and alterations' – a figure which strongly suggests that Fraser, as was common practice in the days of inexpensive printing, used the first proofs more or less as drafts which he could amend freely. Binding seems to have run to a further £250 and lithography to £379. 18, making a total for production of little more than £1300 for 152 copies printed. However, rough jottings assessed the whole cost of the volumes variously at £3150 and £3458. 11. 2.[1] Expenses were of course spread over several years and payments were likewise made piecemeal as Fraser approached his clients so that he could recoup his outlays: the *Buccleuch* volumes were issued in 1878 and the cost from 1873 to 1881 was £2857. 15. 6.[2] The *Douglas Book*, over no less than twenty years (1866–1886), accounted for £3,635. 14. 2, including a payment of £500 to Constables for printing and miscellaneous payments for engravings, as well as fees to Henry Ellis, James Gordon, Mr John Anderson and W.O. Hewlett for transcribing. The total for *Wemyss*, from 1880 to 1889, was £3,267. 3. 9., for *Annandale*, from 1886 to 1896, £3,499. 4 and for *Elphinstone*, from 1893 to 1898, £2,684. 11. 7. The last account was not settled until after Fraser's death, when his executors were involved.[3] Sometimes Fraser asked for relatively

small sums, perhaps as a rule for items not directly
related to volumes in the course of preparation. Thus in
May 1875 he sent Lord Lothian copies of portraits of the
Earl of Ancram 'from Lord Saltoun's original' and of Cecil
Drury from Lord Polwarth's miniature, with a request for
£20 for the two, and he also asked for 2 guineas for
repairing a copy of the 'Confession of Faith' – presumably
the National Covenant – which Lothian had lent to Fraser,
and £7. 17. 6 for a lithograph of the foundation charter
of Newbattle: he added a request for £50 for himself in
respect of 'the expense which I have incurred for the
proposed Cartulary of Jedburgh'.[4]    But Fraser could ask
for much more substantial sums for expenses which had,
he said, overstretched his resources: in March 1880 he
asked Buccleuch for £500: 'I am rather too much in
advance for my small way and I have been overdrawing
my Bank account. This is such a rare occurrence with me
that it affords my Banker some amusement at my expense
of five per cent and they encourage me to continue over-
drafts as they think me a safe customer. But I dislike it'.[5]

In his early days, at least, Fraser claimed that his
charges were moderate when he was engaged to act in
Peerage cases. In 1847, in connection with the Glencairn
peerage, he wrote to Sir Thomas Montgomery Cunninghame
of Corsehill, Bart., assuring him that he would not 'spend
a sixpence beyond what I found to be absolutely necessary
for making out your case as economically and expeditious-
ly as possible', and added: 'In other Peerage claims the
parties allowed me the most uncontrolled latitude in the
management. and in every instance I have acknowledge-
ments of satisfaction and success'.[6]  In 1850 he remarked:
'Last week I had a settlement with the Hyndford claimant,
and he wrote me that my account was "exemplary
moderate"'.[7]  Even so, there could be nothing like a standard charge, when the amount of work varied enormously:
whereas the Herries case cost only about £1000, Fraser
estimated that the Montrose claim would cost £14,000.[8]

Later on, when the family histories were in full
flood, and Fraser's reputation was so well established,
the attitude of his clients varied from the restive to the
indignant. In 1866 Lord Home enquired of Buccleuch how
many copies of the *Buccleuch Book* Fraser had retained for
his own purposes and how much his remuneration had
been.[9]  It does seem that Fraser may not have given
reliable estimates, if estimates at all, and that, during
the long periods when books were in preparation and their
scope sometimes expanded, intermittent payments were made
but no clear picture was evident of the true financial
position. Thus in 1891–2 Fraser had an acrimonious correspondence with the Earl of Haddington, who protested: 'I
must however say that I was rather startled at the cost

of the work, even allowing for the book having assumed larger proportions than was originally intended by you. or arranged for in the written agreement'. and complaint centred in particular on Fraser's personal fees: 'Occupied as above generally described during the preparation in carrying through the work from July 1879 to July 1890 eleven years – in all 1182 days at 21s. per day, £1,241. 2s.'. This suggests that during the eleven years when he was engaged on the book Fraser was devoting a hundred days a year to it, despite his official duties and other private work. Clearly the 'days' cannot all have been full working days by Fraser personally, for much of the labour was that of his clerks, but it is easy to understand why Haddington was 'startled'. He wound up: 'Had I had the least idea that the book would cost me a *third* of the sum ... I should never have undertaken it, because I could not have afforded it. It was only because I believed that your written arrangement brought the cost within such a limit as I could afford. that I consented to go on with the book at all. I cannot assent to protract a settlement of this matter. and still less to burden my successor with it'. He offered to pay £844. 8. 6 at once or to refer the matter to arbitration. 'I can do nothing more, being advised not to acquiesce to your terms.'[10]

There was similar correspondence over Sutherland in 1894-5. The third Duke died in 1892, the year when the book was issued, and the financial settlement was a matter for his agents. who seem to have believed that the distribution of copies was a matter for them and not for Fraser and who objected to a final demand for £113. 12. 2, which they considered should have been covered in the main by a payment of £2008 made in October 1894.[11]  A present of *Haddington* and other works, as a kind of sweetener, was rejected, for in September 1895 Sutherland's agent proposed to return 'the works you sent me which I accepted at the time as a personal mark of kindly feeling but which under present circumstances it would not be agreeable or becoming in me to retain'.[12] Lord Lothian, the good friend who had been the grateful recipient of so many volumes and never had the experience of paying for a family history, was sympathetic to Fraser. He wrote on 22 July 1893: 'I am distressed about the Sutherland Book. Surely as soon as the question of ownership is decided, there will be no difficulty about payment of anything that is due for all your labours'; and in the following February he added: 'I wonder what has happened about your Duke – whose book (or rather yours) was impounded by the widow Duchess? I hope you have managed to arrange it all'.[13]  Fraser viewed complaints with pained astonishment: 'All the other Dukes and noblemen in

Scotland by whom I have been largely employed in similar work invariably treated me with great kindness, courtesy and consideration.[14]

There was a posthumous debate over the cost of the latest of the family histories, *Elphinstone*, which had been issued only in the year before Fraser's death. In June 1898, three months after he died, Lord Elphinstone's agents wrote to Fraser's Trustees regarding the account for the preparation of the book, which was summarised as follows:

| | | | |
|---|---|---|---|
| Time of William Fraser and assistants | £1796. | 0. | 6 |
| Correspondence | 26. | 15. | 0 |
| Expenses | 136. | 19. | 8 |
| Printing etc. | 723. | 18. | 7 |
| | 2683. | 13. | 9 |

Whereof £200 had been paid to account. The agents expressed surprise at the amount of the account, and it was explained — somewhat lamely, it would seem — that initially the book was to be 'an inexpensive one' but that Fraser had changed his plans and increased the size. However, it was agreed to make a deduction of £500 from the total.[15]

Lothian's cordiality seems on the whole to have been more typical of Fraser's relations with his clients than his friction with Haddington and Sutherland. With Lothian he enjoyed something approaching friendship, with little trace of patronage on the Marquis's side. Correspondence with the 8th Marquis started at least as early as 1855 and continued with him and his successor to the end of Fraser's life. The 9th Marquis evidently took a real interest in historical matters outwith those relating to his own family and Fraser from time to time kept him informed not only about the progress of the family histories but also about titbits of information which cropped up in the course of his work. While books went to Lothian from Fraser, the Marquis reciprocated with presents of game: in November 1870 Fraser wrote: 'I am much gratified by your kind remembrance of game, which arrived in excellent condition', and in September 1872 he made a similar acknowledgment.[16] There were invitations too, which Fraser sometimes had to decline, as in September 1875, when Lothian wrote: 'I am sorry you will not be here this season, but I can imagine your interest in the operations at Dingwall'.[17] In November 1882 Lothian asked Fraser to come to Newbattle for the weekend 'to meet several noble lords, some of whom I know you would like to meet'.[18] Buccleuch equalled Lothian in generosity with game: Fraser acknowledged 'your kind remembrance of game' in October 1881, 'a kind present of game' in February 1884 and 'a princely supply of feathers' in December 1885.[19] Invitations as well as presents came from Buccleuch as they did from Lothian, and when there was competition between a Duke and a Marquis for his company Fraser must have felt gratified indeed: in January 1871 Lothian wrote from Newbattle; 'I had hoped to see you at Dalkeith on Sunday and to try to persuade you to come here next Sunday, but find you are due at Dalkeith then and so cannot come here'.[20] They were not the only peers to vie for the great man's attention. In September 1880 Fraser excused himself from an excursion to Lothian's house at Newbattle on Saturday, as Lord and Lady Lindsay had invited him to Kilconquhar for the weekend, and added, 'This request was reinforced by a supply of fur and feather, and I could not well refuse as I was not able to accept last year'.[21]

When Fraser made his will, on 11 December 1896,[22] he allotted £25,000 to the University of Edinburgh for the endowment of 'an additional chair in connection with what may be considered my life work' or a 'chair or professorship of Ancient History with special reference to Palaeography or the science of ancient writings and also with reference to the historical records and charters of the royal, noble and baronial families and the Royal Burghs of Scotland or of other countries, to be called the Sir William Fraser Professorship of Ancient History and Palaeography'; £10,000 'for the purposes of the Library of the said University', partly for the salaries of library staff; £25,000 for 'the endowment of homes for the poor in the city or county of Edinburgh' including preferentially 'those who may be ascertained to be authors or artists and who either from non-success in the profession or work of literature or of art or from whatever cause are in necessitous circumstances'; £15.000 for his sister: and the residue (including the £15,000 set aside for his sister should she predecease him, or after her death should she survive him) to be divided between the Royal Infirmary of Edinburgh and the University (especially for bursaries in connection with history or studentships for promoting research) but 'if thought proper a portion of the said funds should be applied towards the expense of publishing original works in connection with historical subjects'. Fraser was thus confident that he had at his disposal a sum well in excess of £75,000. and when his estate came to be settled after his death its total value was £104,728. 17s. 1d., which, (especially after allowing for the incidence of taxation) must have been worth more than £2,000,000 would be worth today.[23]

Fraser's bequests gave rise to various complications.
So far as the University was concerned, there was
discussion about the rights of the Senatus (as opposed to
the Court) to accept and administer the bequest and about
the rights of the Trustees to consider the Deed of Foundation of the Chair; reference had to be made to the Court
of Session on the obligations of the Trustees and the
Senatus. [24] Apart from such technicalities, there was debate
within the University as to the interpretation of Fraser's
terminology. Everyone who knew Fraser and studied the
words he used in his will and elsewhere knew that by
Ancient History he meant medieval Scottish History, but he
had said 'Ancient History', which was open to another
interpretation. When, in March 1899, a Joint Committee of
Court and Senatus reported, it recommended that the new
Chair should be mainly and primarily concerned with early
Scottish history and palaeography but should include the
early history and palaeography of other countries. The
Court approved, but a formal dissent was recorded in the
names of Professors Butcher and Crum Brown, who held
that 'Ancient History' should have 'the sense in which the
phrase is known to the English language'. After a lapse
of nearly two years, in December 1900, the Court resolved,
on the request of Senatus, to institute a lectureship in
Greek and Roman History from a portion of the residue of
Fraser's bequest, with at least £150 to the lecturer. [25] The
Chair was filled by the appointment of Peter Hume Brown
in July 1901, [26] and for half a century there existed a
Professor of Ancient (Scottish) History and Palaeography
and a Lecturer in Ancient (Greek and Roman) History.
When a change was made to the simple 'Scottish History'
Professor Dickinson was prevailed on, at the last minute,
not to recommend the dropping of the mention of 'Palaeo-
graphy'. So far as the amount Fraser had destined for the
Library was concerned, £3000 was to be used for making
a catalogue of the Library. [27]

Little time seems to have been lost in proceeding with
the erection of the Fraser Homes at Colinton. The architect
was Arthur Balfour Paul, a son of Sir James Balfour Paul,
Lord Lyon, and when they were opened on 2 March 1901
J.R. Macphail, a Trustee, declared very appropriately that
'They have got here something in keeping with the life-
work of Sir William Fraser: something of the old Scottish
style, which would be an adornment to the village in which
it was situated, as well as a comfortable home to the in-
mates'. [28] I have sometimes remarked that it was a pity
that Fraser did not think of earmarking one of those very
attractive residences for a retired holder of his Chair: but
his £25,000 sufficed to provide a professorial salary which
then was almost princely and he would not have thought

that one of the modest houses in the Homes would be appropriate. Ultimately the Trustees found that Fraser's bequest was inadequate to maintain the Homes, and most of the responsibility for them passed to the Merchant Company in 1960. but the Trustees still nominate to six of the houses and dispense certain gifts to the inhabitants.

Fraser received honours as well as material rewards, perhaps partly because his influential acquaintances among the nobility said a word at an appropriate point. When. in 1882, the University of Edinburgh conferred on him the honorary degree of LL.D., Lord Rosebery, the Liberal politician, was Rector, and it was a Liberal Prime Minister, Gladstone, under whom Fraser was created a Companion of the Order of the Bath in 1885. But in 1887. when Lord Lothian was Secretary for Scotland, it was a Conservative Premier, Salisbury, who wrote to Fraser informing him that the Queen had been 'pleased to give expression to the high esteem in which your literary and official labours are held both by herself and the public generally by conferring upon you a Civil Knight Commandership of the Bath'. Fraser was invested by the Queen at Osborne on 2 August, according to the inscription on an empty case, in the possession of Tods, Murray and Jamieson, which once contained the insignia of the Order. Fraser's noble patrons were no doubt drawn from both political parties. The knighthood was an unique distinction for a Scottish historian, for, while English historians are knighted almost as a matter of routine and occasionally attain peerages, only one Professor of Scottish History has become a knight, and that was Sir Robert Rait. who was so honoured in his capacity as Principal of the University of Glasgow.

The honours which came to Fraser were appropriate in view of the place of his writings in Scottish historiography. Thanks largely to Thomas Thomson and Sir Walter Scott. a massive programme of the publication of source material, from the national records and other repositories. had been launched early in the nineteenth century, but still better was to come. It was only after 1870 that the official publication of public records really got into its stride. and at the same point the Historical MSS Commission started on its task of informing us about non-public records. The years from 1870 to 1914 stand out as a kind of peak, the phase to which we owe the bulk of the printed records we constantly use. The succession of scholarly writers and editors continued too – David Laing, Cosmo Innes. Hill Burton and W.F. Skene among them. While Fraser was not responsible for much if any initiation in official publication, the period of his tenure of the office of Deputy Keeper was the most productive period

which record publication has ever seen or is ever likely
to see. His own fifty volumes of family books added
enormously to the amount of material that was available
from private records, to supplement public records. The
industry and productivity of the Victorians is something
at which one never ceases to marvel. One cannot look at
Fraser's notes – even at the little which is extant–or at
the evidence he gave in peerage cases, or at his
correspondence, without feeling uncomfortably that an
enormous amount of labour must have been duplicated and
that the answers to many questions which have been raised
repeatedly in later years and still crop up today could be
found somewhere in the output of Fraser and his contemporaries.

Fraser had the gratification of enjoying something
approaching adulation in his own day, as an anonymous
article in the *Dundee Advertiser* of 1 June 1896:

> There is no Scotsman living who has so much ex-
> perience in deciphering ancient documents, nor one
> who can so skilfully extract information from faded
> and time-worn parchments. In this kind of work he
> has spent half-a-century of his life, and has ac-
> complished more than any of his contemporaries in his
> own line.... His wide acquaintance with charters and
> documents in private repositories put him in a
> position to quote precedents that are not always
> recorded in official books on Peerage law; and his
> phenomenally retentive memory enabled him often to
> bring up the proper reference at the required moment.
> He was thus an invaluable witness in cases of con-
> tested Peerages, and during more than forty years he
> was frequently summoned to London to give evidence
> before the Committee for Privileges of the House of
> Lords, to whom the decision of such cases is com-
> mitted. Sir William was regarded as an authority in
> matters of this kind, having acquired special know-
> ledge, which placed him in an exceptional position.
> On questions involving genealogical research he has
> been considered as without a rival: for the untying
> of the Gordian knot of the marriages and inter--
> marriages among the Scottish nobility, puzzling as
> these are even to the practical genealogist, is a
> simple task to one who carries the history of the
> noble families of Scotland in his head, and has the
> dates of the leading events at his finger--ends. In
> this department of knowledge it will not be easy to
> supply the place of Sir William Fraser.... Sir William
> Fraser, despite his advanced age, has not yet laid
> aside his pen. It may safely be said that there is no
> living Scottish writer who has done so much to put to

flight the vain imaginings of pseudo–historical writers
as Sir William Fraser has done. Family historians,
following his example, no longer find their materials
in the absurdly romantic traditions of a locality.
They search for solid facts amongst the documents in
charter–rooms and private repositories. By a careful
examination of contemporary documents experts can
often settle the age of a charter though it bear no
clearly expressed date. The puzzling caligraphy of early documents can now be read off as easily as nineteenth century manuscript – sometimes more easily,
indeed, than the characterless type–writing of our day.
Foolish traditions are relegated to the nursery and
truth is literally found to be stranger than fiction.
The age of the ignorant credulity in this sphere is
passing away: the age of rational faith has already
begun.
The writer of those lines possessed an optimism about the
triumph of truth over fiction which now, after nearly
another century, seems nothing less than fatuous. But the
article at least demonstrates that Fraser had friends and
admirers among his contemporaries.

# CHAPTER 10

## FRASER IN CONTROVERSY

Reference has recently been made to 'the appalling lack of public manners' as 'the scourge of the historical profession' in the 1980s,[1] but few recent writers, however profound their disagreements, have mounted such displays of ferocity as Fraser's critics did a century and more earlier. They had opportunities not so readily available now, because, when scholars were comparatively affluent and printing costs were low, material could be privately printed which would be unacceptable nowadays to either a commercial publisher or an editor. Whether Fraser felt that he had no case or felt that he could proceed serenely on his profitable operations in defiance of criticism, he was not much given to answering back, and so far as civility goes he compares favourably with his detractors.

His chief antagonists were two men of different types. John Riddell (1785–1862), an advocate, was one of the most thorough and scholarly of writers on Scottish peerage law, his opinions on which have continued to be treated with respect. Mark Napier (1798–1879) was also an advocate, who made wide use of source material in his writings, but he was no record scholar and was an opinionated, some might say bigoted, adherent of the broadly conservative side in Scotland's past – royalist, Jacobite, Episcopalian – and controversy on behalf of such lost causes was the breath of his nostrils. While Riddell and Napier both attacked Fraser, they also quarrelled between themselves, so the debate could be three-sided.

The principal areas of contention focussed in one way or another on the history of the Lennox and the related matter of the muniments of the Duke of Montrose. Riddell, the eldest of the three writers, was to be known as an adherent of Lord Lindsay, for whom in 1845 he established a right to the earldom of Crawford and whose claim to the ancient dukedom of Montrose he supported in opposition to Fraser in 1850. But he had been on the scene as early as 1828, with a *Reply to the Mis-statements of Dr Hamilton of Bardowie ... with Remarks on the claim of the Lennoxes of Woodhead to the male representation ... of the original Earls of Lennox*. Napier entered the field in 1834 with his

*Memoir of John Napier of Merchiston*, in   which   he   ranged
widely, and next year, in a *History   of   the   Partition   of
the Lennox*, he  put  forward  a  claim  of  the  Napier family
to be heirs to the Lennox earldom. Riddell, who supported
a claim by the Haldanes, as senior to the Napier line, at
once retorted. His *Tracts, Legal and Historical* (1835), contained 'Observations upon the representation of the Rusky
and Lennox families and other points in Mr Napier's
Memoirs of Merchiston', and he followed this, still in the
same year, with *Additional Remarks upon the Question of
the Lennox and Rusky Representation in answer to the
author of the* 'History of the Partition of the Lennox'. The
latter was a slashing attack on Napier, who, it was
shown, could not translate even  stereotyped Latin phrases
and of whom Riddell remarked, 'The learned gentleman, if
we may use the phrase, seems to have become intoxicated
by the mere sound of his words'.

Fraser's first family book, *The   Stirlings   of   Keir*,
came out in 1858, and Riddell challenged him, as he had
challenged Napier in the Lennox case. over the advocacy
of the claims of one branch of a family over another. In
*Comments in refutation of pretensions advanced for the
first time and statements in a recent work 'The Stirlings
of Keir and their Family Papers' (1860)*, Fraser was deno-
unced for carelessness and misrepresentation.

The long-drawn-out Mar case, which really extended
from 1866 to 1875 and attracted uncommon interest, was one
on which every antiquary and genealogist probably had
his views, and Napier's seem to have been contrary to
Fraser's. He alluded to the matter in his *Memorie* of his
mother's paternal lineage (1872) and several years later
he wrote: 'Lord Stair asked me the other day what my
opinion of the Marr case was and I said it was a shame-
ful miscarriage of justice; a downright robbery'.[2]

The most bitter dispute arose after Fraser published
his *Lennox* (1874), in the Preface to which both Riddell
and Napier were criticised. It appears that when Fraser
began to prepare his *Lennox* for publication he asked for
the loan of woodcuts or other illustrations which Napier
had used, and the request was refused. Yet, when
Fraser's volume appeared, Napier 'entertained the con-
viction', so his son Francis asserted, that 'certain
illustrations in the second volume of "The Lennox" had
been copied by a photographic process from the "Memoirs
of John Napier of Merchiston" without his permission, and,
indeed, against his wishes, which he had made known to
Mr Fraser'. And, Francis Napier added, 'If my father was
in error ... it is open to him [Fraser] to explain in what
manner those illustrations were obtained'.[3]   Mark Napier's
full-scale attack, in *The Lanox of Auld*, a   150-page   re-

view of Fraser's work, was written in 1875 but not published until 1880, the year after Napier's death. It appears that Fraser had approached Napier's publishers with a threat of legal action should the review be published, and that Lord Napier and perhaps other friends had pleaded with Mark to modify his tone, but this he refused to do. In a letter dated 19 March 1879 Mark Napier wrote to Lord Napier on this topic and also on the *Buccleuch* Book (1878), where Fraser had given further offence to Mark Napier through the Napier connection with the Scotts of Thirlestane:

> And how solemn you are, – 'And now the time has come to bury the hatchet and to mitigate any expressions of ridicule which the proof sheets of Lanox of Auld may contain'.... I would, however, rather bite Fraser than be bitten by him. But I choose neither to be Fraser–bitten nor flea–bitten. His last book [Buccleuch] was wanted and is very acceptable to me ..., but as for the landscape gardening part of it it is as you say too dumpy and gaudy and as for historical value as regards Border history, or the history of Scotland ... almost useless as a book for consultation by literary students.... Bury the hatchet quotha? Why, there is a hatchet against some one or thing in every page of my book so I would have to bury four hundred hatchets.... Is it not funny in Fraser to write me that friendly note, after having bullied my publisher behind my back with a threat of an action of damages for publishing an hypothetical libel against him.... I dare not look into the book [*Buccleuch*] as yet, but Charlotte [Mark's wife] pointed out the notice of Thirlestane to me, in which he vouchsafes to favour us ... with a *may be* that we are come of Buccleuch, and a branch not without its own romance – which he instances by that 'interesting' tradition of the murder of young Thirlestane ... – perfect rubbish, of which I published a crushing refutation ... in Dr Marshall's 'Genealogist' in London.[4]

Subsequently (on Easter Day, 13 April), Napier wrote again to Lord Napier:

> Touching the 'Scotts of Buccleuch' by William Fraser, I have dipped very little into it and only found what disgusts me more and more at his ignorance, vanity and presumption. Some days ago I drove to the Royal Register House to hunt for something there and had a long confab with Mr Dickson. the Keeper of the Historical Department. I found him highly indignant at the 'author' of the Scotts of Buccleuch.... Mr Dickson asked me if I had seen a review of the book

in the Dumfries Standard. I told him that two copies of it had been sent me. I did not know by whom. but that I did not read a line of either, taking it for granted to be a puff of Fraser written by himself; that I had heard afterwards that it was against him rather, but still I had not read it. Dickson then told me that it was such an exposure of him that Fraser was very angry about it and most anxious that it should not get abroad: so much so. that (I think but must ascertain the fact with more certainty) he went to Mr Burnet the Lord Lyon to intreat him not to disseminate the paper. If this be the fact the Lyon must have written the article – but when I was about to inquire I found poor Burnet had been attacked with typhoid .... But this is not all my story. Mr Dickson told me that a very excellent and learned person of the name of Armstrong had for years been occupied in researches on the subject of the Border families and this with the view of publication and that his collection was valuable. Being interested of course in the Duke's book [i.e. *Buccleuch*] he frankly put Fraser in possession of the whole of his stores – and all the thanks he has got is that they have been all appropriated without a word of acknowledgment from Fraser in any shape. Now this Mr Armstrong is a very unpresuming and high-minded person and he came to the Keeper of the Historical Room in great distress for fear that the article in the Standard should be attributed to him .... I find that the article (which I have now read) concludes with this sentence: 'We may mention here that the work is enriched from the voluminous manuscript notes, the result of many years research, of Mr R.B. Armstrong, who generously placed his valuable collection at the disposal of the author. It is usual to acknowledge contributions of this nature in the preface. but this has been overlooked'. I am not surprised that Mr Armstrong should be annoyed at the idea of the article, with its concluding complaint. being attributed to him. But he is not the less offended with Mr Fraser and it has determined him (as Mr Dickson tells me) to publish his collections, for his own protection. I asked Mr Dickson how soon this could be done: he says it will take a twelve month. That article in the Standard has opened my eyes wider to what I had some suspicion of, that Fraser's own researches and originality of matter in this last gold coach of his is not a fig's worth.... Mr Dickson also told me that all the learned references and evidences of research that appear at the foot of his pages are taken from Mr

Armstrongs collections, although they appear as his own. Faugh !

It appears by a puff and extracts in the Edinburgh Courant that some friend has reviewed in the Edinburgh Review, 1st article, his Lennox book with a tremendous puff of himself.... I have reviewed that book by anticipation. When I read that in the Courant ... I immediately instructed my publisher to advertise in the Courant and two Dumfries papers 'Nearly ready etc. etc. etc. The Lanox of Auld ...'[5]

When R.B. Armstrong published the first (and only) volume of his *History of Liddesdale, Eskdale, Ewesdale, Wauchopdale and the Debatable Land* in 1883, he acknowledged permission from Fraser to consult a printed Calendar of the Maxwell and Herries Muniments, and went on: 'Before concluding this short preface, it is perhaps necessary to make the following statement. In the year 1878 *The Scotts of Buccleuch* by Mr William Fraser appeared, containing a considerable amount of matter relating to Liddesdale and the Debateable Land; and as it might otherwise be supposed that the author had failed to acknowledge some indebtedness to a work issued previously to his own, he thinks it right to explain that the greater portion of the transcripts and notes which he had before that period made for the purposes of this work were placed at Mr Fraser's disposal and largely used by him'.[6]

Mark Napier had not been deflected either by pleas to bury the hatchet or by gifts from Fraser of *Buccleuch* and *The Lennox*. His thanks for the latter, he said, were due not to Fraser but to 'the late Mr Oswald of Auchincruive', for Oswald (whose claim to a descent from the Haldanes was proved by Fraser from papers at Buchanan Castle) had indeed commissioned the preparation of *The Lennox* and was reasonably described as Fraser's 'patron in this undertaking'. In *The Lanox of Auld* Napier scoffed at Fraser as 'a sort of landscape gardener among antiquarian family bibliographers' and complained that the work was 'not a family book at all.' He quoted parallel passages in his own earlier work and Fraser's *Lennox* to support the accusation that Fraser had plagiarised the text of the *Partition* as well as Napier's illustrations.

Napier had entered a different field, and one in which he could perhaps be more damaging to Fraser, by criticising the latter's operations for the Historical MSS. Commission. In 1872 he printed *A letter to Sir William Stirling Maxwell, Bart., one of the Commissioners appointed under the Royal Commission for the discovery of latent historical MSS., tendering a respectful remonstrance against the Royal Commissioners reporting to Her Majesty and publishing abbreviates of royal letters and other MSS.*

as of new historical materials discovered under the
auspices of the Royal Commission which have been previously published in extenso and have in other hands fulfilled
the purposes of history. He pointed out (p. 5) that the
Secretary had instructed the Inspectors that 'the object of
the Commission is *solely* the discovery of *unknown* historical
and literary materials'. This was a preliminary to an
attack on Fraser's *Montrose Report*, in which he pointed
out *inter alia* that he (Napier) had printed a lot of the
papers relating to the Great Marquis of Montrose twenty
years before and that some of the papers noticed by
Fraser had been printed even earlier. It would appear
that Napier was prepared to go even further, and bluntly
accuse Fraser of making a Calendar of the Montrose
muniments at the public expense, but Fraser commented,
'This was so absurd that I made him suppress his
pamphlet at his peril, and I have heard no more of it.
His imprudence often betrays him into very improper
language'.[7]

It should, however, be added that, long after the
criticism of Fraser's Royal Commission proceedings, and
long after the row over *The Lennox*, when *Buccleuch* was received by Napier, shortly before his death, he congratulated Fraser on his work.[8]

Fraser's relations with Riddell extended to matters
unconnected with the Lennox and Montrose issues. In 1842,
when Riddell was fifty-seven and an advocate of thirty-
five years' standing, Fraser, only twenty-seven and not
yet even an S.S.C., was engaged in the Marchmont case
and wrote to his senior in a rather lofty tone, thanking
him for information received, explaining that it was not
possible to retain any other counsel in the case but
intimating that if Riddell supplied further information he
would be rewarded.[9] From later correspondence it appears
that Riddell was believed to have retained certain papers
belonging to the Douglas charter chest, which was Lord
Home's property, and this caused embarrassment to
Riddell's patron Lord Lindsay, who acquired Riddell's MSS
with a view to presenting them to the Advocates' Library.
'We can have no positive proof'. wrote Lord Home, 'that
Mr Riddell kept the documents back; but as in the Pollok
case', it is admitted that the probabilities were all that
way'.[10] Fraser told Lord Lindsay, 'If I saw the papers in
question I think I could say at once if they belong to the
Douglas charter chest and I trust that your lordship may
consider yourself entitled to restore them to it'.[11] Lindsay
explained the position to Maidment, a well-known antiquary: Fraser claimed on behalf of Lord Home, and with
Lord Home's sanction, as husband of Lady Home, the heir

of line of the Douglases of Angus, certain letters from Nos. 15 and 114 of the series of the Riddell Papers, as described in the printed catalogue, and also a notebook containing an account of deeds in the Douglas charter chest which Fraser thought Riddell had obtained from that repository and not returned and which must consequently be among the 'Riddell Papers' bought by Lindsay; Lindsay had bought the papers on the understanding that he would bequeath them to the Advocates' Library and could not act without the consent of the Curators of that Library.[12] After consideration by Fraser, a representative of Lord Home and the Curators of the Library, the papers were returned to Lord Home.[13] In view of the mass of papers, from diverse sources, which were to turn up among Fraser's own possessions, it is a little ironical to find him at this point cast in the role of the defender of the integrity of a charter chest.

The critic of Fraser who most happily combined scholarship with urbanity was George Burnett, Lyon King of Arms and editor of over a dozen volumes of *The Exchequer Rolls of Scotland* published between 1878 and 1893. In 1881 he printed *The Red Book of Menteith reviewed*, in the form of a letter to Fraser, extending to 67 pages. *Menteith* had been published in 1880, the year which saw also the publication of volumes iii and iv of the *Exchequer Rolls*, bringing the series down to 1436 and containing, as was then the custom, long introductions in which the editor ranged widely over the history of the period. The matters of historical fact and interpretation on which Burnett and Fraser differed were too numerous and complex to be recounted here, but they were related to questions as to which of the two had the better claim to originality and which of the two had made the prior discovery of certain source material. Fraser had clearly profited from Burnett's work – not only text, but introductions – and had, for example, recast the account of the family of Murdoch, Duke of Albany, which he had given in *The Lennox*, and produced a revised version in *Menteith*; but, while Fraser had criticised Burnett's introduction to *Exchequer Rolls* iv, he had evidently drawn lavishly on Burnett's introductions without acknowledgment: Burnett declared that he had readily given help to Fraser and had been promised a copy of *Menteith* in recognition. Fraser had accused Burnett of printing or referring to documents in the Register House as if he had discovered them, when they had already been printed or known to Fraser, while Burnett accused Fraser of making excessive claims to originality in discovering documents which Burnett had already seen. It seems reasonable to suggest that Fraser adopted an unduly proprietory attitude to

material which was, after all, public record and not
likely to have been totally unknown to previous scholars,
including the office staff. Burnett said that Fraser had
ignored information available in such obvious places as
Burke's *Landed Gentry* and he rebuked him for showing
imperfect knowledge of the nature of fourteenth–century
peerages by writing in *Menteith* that Sir Robert Graham
'continued a Commoner for several years and until the
coronation of his father as King Robert II. From and after
that ceremony he was Earl of Menteith'. Burnett addressed
Fraser thus: 'Peers and Commoners! my dear Mr Fraser.
There were no more Peers and Commoners in those days
than there were cavaliers and roundheads. steam engines.
school boards or peerage–earldoms'. It was characteristic
of Burnett to adopt a light–handed approach, of which
there are other instances. *'En revanche* for the charge of
filching from you one daughter of Albany, I am in a
position to prove that you have kidnapped from me another
daughter of the same royal Duke'. And again, 'That you
should have changed your mind as to the paternity of
Arthur and Walter [sons of Duke Murdoch] between 1874
and 1881 is nothing out of the way: but that you have
changed it between page 278 and page 280 can, I fancy,
only be accounted for by the untoward accident by which
your book. though in type before mine, was published
after it'.

   Fraser was on the whole probably far too fully
occupied with his peerage cases and his family histories
to be readily diverted into anything that could be called
pamphleteering. In 1850, however, he prepared a vindi-
cation of Sir Patrick Home of Polwarth (1641–1724) against
the charges made by Lord Macaulay, who called him 'a
man incapable alike of leading and of following, conceit-
ed, captious, and wrongheaded, an endless talker, a
sluggard in action against the enemy and active only
against his own allies'. Controversy with Napier and
others was carried on in the pages of *The Spectator*. An article compared the Scotts of Buccleuch to moss–troopers on
a grand scale, and Fraser defended them in a letter to
the Duke,[14] but Fraser went into print in *The Spectator*  on
the record of the Scotts and the question whether the
Buccleuch of 1513 had been at Flodden. [15]

   The criticism to which Fraser had exposed himself at
the hands of Armstrong and Dickson. and perhaps Burnett,
probably affected his standing with other historians more
than Napier's attacks did. That there was a certain cool-
ness is the most likely explanation of the absence of
Fraser's name from the list of members of the Scottish
History Society, founded in 1886.

# CHAPTER 11

## FRASER'S PAPERS

Fraser's sister, who had kept house for him since 1846, died on 21 December 1897 and he survived her until only 13 March 1898. Death may have come with little warning, or at any rate in circumstances which did not permit or encourage him to wind up his affairs, with the result that his Trustees had to deal with a large residue of papers on which he was working or hoped to work or which he had simply neglected to return to their owners. Working as he had done under great pressure, he could have been excused for sometimes losing sight of material and not sending it back as he should have done. But the man was clearly something of a magpie, who can hardly be acquitted of retaining papers which came into his hands in one way or another but had never become his property in any formal way. His motive was not material gain, for there is no evidence that he sold or hoped to sell them, but the explanation is not mere absent-mindedness either. It was not that he thought of filching documents which might be regarded as showpieces or which had great historical value, but he probably liked to have old MSS under his hand and he was something of a collector in practice if not by deliberate intent. In his later years he seems even to have failed to turn over to the Register House, as he would have done earlier, some official records which he had come on in private collections – not only a protocol book, but volumes of the Treasurer's Accounts. All in all, whether through carelessness. absent-mindedness or reluctance to part with things, there was a mass of assorted material in his possession at his death. There is a list, drawn up for his Trustees, of no less than eighty 'charter collections' or muniments which had been in his hands, and a Memorandum of December 1898 states that 'Sir William had in his possession at the time of his death a large number of collections of muniments and documents belonging to a number of Scottish families, the task of arranging which, with a view to their being returned to their owners, has been one of exceptional difficulty'.[1]

The 'task of arranging' the mass of material could hardly be overtaken either by the Trustees personally or by their law agents. All four of the 'assistants' or clerks who had been in Fraser's employment on his decease seem to have been kept on until the beginning of 1899, for on 6 February of that year payments were made to Scott of 250 guineas, Gibb 150, MacLeod 75 and Buchanan 25, presumably for varying periods of service; and Gibb was kept on for the better part of another twelve months.[2] Two of the Trustees – Balfour Paul and Macphail – did, indeed, take an active part, and were suitably rewarded: Balfour Paul received 250 guineas for his help in examining books and MSS, late in 1899, and Macphail (under whose direction W.K. Dickson had been commissioned to make a calendar of certain material in 1901) received 250 guineas in 1913 when he produced two MS books listing Fraser papers and offering guidance as to their disposal.[3] The bulk of the material which had come from private owners (and which was usually easily identifiable as to ownership) was returned in the course of 1898 and 1899, but the residue continued to give intermittent trouble to the Trustees and their agents (Tods, Murray and Jamieson) from that point almost to the present.

Among the major collections which were easily identifiable were nineteen boxes of Annandale Papers, although the *Annandale Book* had been printed in 1894. More surprisingly, although the *Buccleuch Book* had been issued in 1878, when Fraser died there was still Buccleuch material in his possession and in 1899 his Trustees prepared an explanatory memorandum. Eight charter boxes, after having their contents checked and arranged, were now ready to be returned to Dalkeith. They included transcripts of 20 volumes of Queensberry letters of the period 1663–1705, made by Fraser for Buccleuch in 1867–73: they had been sent to Dalkeith but had been returned to Fraser in 1873 so that he could report on them for the Historical MSS Commission and at the time of Fraser's death were still 'being reported on'.[4] A similar situation arose over Lothian muniments. The Trustees had to make a 'Statement of evidence shewing the purpose for which the charter muniments of the Marquis of Lothian, K.T., were delivered to Sir William Fraser, K.C.B. and also shewing for what purposes he retained them in his possession until the time of his death in March 1898'. There was a tin chest containing charters and miscellaneous papers, a smallwood box containing transcripts of writs, a parcel of five copies of *Ancram–Lothian Correspondence* and several parcels of lithographs of charters. Fraser had received the two boxes in 1860 and 1878 and the *Ancram–Lothian Correspondence* in 1879. All were ready for return to Lothian on 2 March 1899

and according to a draft receipt were received in 1900.[5]
There exist receipts for papers, including letters of Sir
Walter Scott, which had been borrowed by Fraser at
various dates from 1862 to 1889 and apparently were all
still in his possession at the time of his death.[6]

The return of private muniments to the homes from
which they had come was correct procedure. but it is
difficult to see why twenty letters from W.E. Gladstone
were sent to John R. Gladstone in April 1898. because. as
the letters had presumably been written to Fraser they
were Fraser archives and not Gladstone archives.[7] Some
other odd decisions were made in efforts to find appropriate destinations for various items as the years went
on. In 1912 an extract decreet by John Spottiswoode,
'provinciall' [that is, superintendent] of Lothian for
reduction of a process of heresy against Sir James Hamilton
of Kincavill was presented to the Assembly Hall Library at
the Tolbooth Church, titles of the lands of Idvies went to
the Earl of Southesk and a Disposition by Thomas
Ruddiman went to the Advocates' Library, presumably
because Ruddiman had once been Keeper there.[8] In 1926 a
Speech by General Monck to the Clothworkers' Hall in
London was given to the Clothworkers' Company, Mincing
Lane, three items went to Sir George Stirling of Glorat and
some documents were sent, but only on loan, to Dr W.A.
Macnaughton. D.P.H., Stonehaven.[9] In 1931 an item was
lent to the Naval and Military Museum in Edinburgh Castle
and as late as 1950, when a Commission by Queen Anne
was presented to that repository, various individual items
were still being distributed to appropriate places.[10]

It was only gradually that anything like a policy
emerged, and there seems to have been some hesitation
even about the destination of material which was public
record or properly transmissible to the Register House.
Among the Leven and Melville Papers in Fraser's
possession were eighteen volumes of the Accounts of the
Treasurers of Scotland, presumably retained by Lord
Leven's ancestor when he was Treasurer Depute and
representing a gap in a series housed in the Register
House. The Trustees, when they consulted Dr Maitland
Thomson, the Curator of Historical Records. merely asked
him if he would like them to make 'representations' to
Lord Leven, and the volumes were in fact returned to
private hands, to remain there for many years.[11] In 1903
Tods, Murray and Jamieson handed to the Register House
two volumes of the Burgh Court Book of Inverkeithing and
the Protocol Book of William Veitch, Peebles,[12] but the
Protocol Book of Robert Brown was not transmitted until
1912.[13] It was obviously harder to determine the appropriate
destination for material which was not official record. and

there is evidence of a good deal of what looks like vacillation or indecision. In 1913 the Trustees handed over to the Register House a collection of 'charters' of various dates, and these, along with other small transmissions in 1922, 1926, 1931 and 1934, were together calendared as 'The Fraser Charters', a collection of items ranging in dates from 1233 to 1830. In 1953 the Trustees deposited Lists of Charters in Various Muniment Rooms, which were appended to the Calendar of Fraser Charters.[14]

However, while the Register House was regarded chiefly as the proper repository for the archives of central government and local authorities, for long after Fraser's death documents from private archives tended then to go rather to the Advocates' (later the National) Library. To that institution the Trustees made several transmissions at various dates down to the 1930s, e.g.,

| | | |
|---|---|---|
| NLS MSS | 90 | Papers, all but one printed in *Fraser Papers* (SHS), presented 1926 |
| | 118 | Note Book of brothers of John Home of Blackadder 1664–76, presented 1928 |
| | 137 | Durris Papers 1741–55, presented 1928 |
| | 573 | (i) Letters of Harriet Siddons 1830–33, presented 1930 |
| | 1016 | Transcripts of some Morton Charters, presented 1935 |
| | 1027 | (iv) Tom Purdie's accounts for work done at Abbotsford, 1821, presented 1934 |
| | 1031 | Correspondence and Papers of the Dukes of Hamilton 1627-1809, presented 1931 |
| | 1033 | Correspondence of George Hamilton, Earl of Orkney, 1703-6 |
| | 1034 | Miscellaneous Papers 17th–19th centuries |
| | 1035 | 'Vindication of Sir Patrick Home of Polwarth ... from the charges of Mr Macaulay ... prepared at the request of the Earl of Haddington, the Lord Polwarth and Sir Hugh Hume-Campbell of Marchmont, Bart., by William Fraser, 1850'. Fos. iv, 193. |

The last three were presented in 1934, when, from among the MSS transmitted to the Library by the Trustees, some items were made over to the Register House by Dr Meikle. the Librarian.[15] Later. on 29 May 1947, a parcel of papers was sent by Tods, Murray and Jamieson to Dr Meikle. who deposited it in the Department of MSS.[16] This material, contained in one box (MS TD/171), consists of a collection of autograph letters and other documents, arranged alphabetically from A to L. A description of the contents of this box indicates how wide and varied Fraser's interests had been.

Among the parties are Alexander, Earl of Stirling, 17th century; Sir Andrew Agnew, 1819; Alexander Adam [Rector of High School of Edinburgh]; Lord Annandale 1668; Lord Belhaven; Duke of Buccleuch to Fraser 1857; Countess of Balcarres 1668; Earl of Buchan. relating to repair of Dryburgh Abbey, 1789; Cranston of that ilk; Earl of Perth 1670; Earl of Dunmore 1760s; Lord Lauderdale 1761 and 1769; Earl of Leven 1696; Earl of Callendar 1652; Paper on Lovat Peerage 1839; Lord Livingston of Almond 1672; Lord Hopetoun 1757. There are testimonials, receipts for stipend, tacks, bonds, discharges and other minor deeds, as well as the words of some songs. No doubt some of them were collected as autographs, but it is difficult to detect any rational principle, even regarding them as autographs, for some of the writers were extremely in- significant people. They are almost like a selection of the Miscellanea and Trivia which in any collection of family papers do not readily fit into any category or which it seems unduly troublesome to place in any category. They are mainly of 18th and 19th century dates. but include a deed of 1472 by Robert Crichton of Sanquhar. a copy of a charter of 1509, an instrument of assignation by Richard Simson, citizen of Glasgow, 1544, and documents of 1573, 1583 and 1590. The latest dated item seems to be a letter from Buccleuch to Fraser in 1857, and there is one undated letter to Fraser when he was in the Sasine Office. Only a few seem to relate to Fraser's business, but there are indications of his interest in the Annandale Peerage – a copy of the warrant or signature for a patent creating the Earl of Annandale a Marquis, 24 June 13th year of William III; and 'Excerpt from the inventory of the title deeds of Annandale'.

One curiosity in the collection is this letter, dated at 'Dune', 20 April 1784:

'Sir,

I have it from undoubted authority that you in most officious manner have attempted convince the world that the Marchmont peerage will become extinct after his lordship's death. Know, then, Sir. that what- ever your motive for this impertinent doctrine may be, you have advanced a menifest [sic] falsehood and the period is fast approaching when your assertions will be confuted in the fullest sense and your exertions crowned with similar success to that of a reptile which attempted to sting a rider but spent its poison in the heel of his boot.

Yours etc.
Antiquary'.

This must have come to Fraser's hands in connection with the Marchmont Peerage case, in which he was involved in 1843.

The other half of this alphabetical arrangement constitutes Box 1, folders 3 to 11, in the collection surveyed by the National Register of Archives (Scotland) and now in the Record Office as GD 397, described below.

More Fraser material was to reach the National Library later, but not directly from the Trustees. Indeed, there seems never to have been any clear policy, in the minds of the Trustees or anyone else, for the final destination of Fraser's papers, and in view of their diversified nature that is perhaps hardly surprising. There were indeed Fraser's own 'archives' in the shape of correspondence and accounts relating to his historical work, but the papers *in toto* represented an artificial accumulation, much of it in truth belonging to other archives from which it had been abstracted or at any rate separated. Nor was there, for long after Fraser's death, what would now be called a sufficiently responsible attitude to 'old papers'. Some light is thrown on the situation and the outlook by a letter dated 6 August 1934 from W.K. Dickson, Librarian of the National Library, to 'my dear Innes', the future Sir Thomas Innes of Learney, Lord Lyon. [17] The circumstances were that Sheriff Macphail, who had been one of the Fraser Trustees, died on 15 October 1933. As already mentioned, he had had a hand in arranging some Fraser papers earlier, and on his death there were in his house nine boxes of papers which were the property of the Trustees. On 27 June 1934 the Trustees agreed that this material was to go to the National Library, but was to be examined by Thomas Innes of Learney. [18] In his letter of 6 August, W.K. Dickson explained that he had gone through 'the whole of the Fraser papers which were left in my hands by Macphail', and it is fairly clear that this material was not identical with the 'nine boxes' removed from Macphail's house after his death. The likelihood seems to be that Macphail had been in possession of a considerable amount of Fraser's material, presumably with a view to his making a selection for the Scottish History Society volume which he edited for issue in 1924. Dickson went on, with reference to the papers 'left in his hands by Macphail';

> I have handed over to Douglas Dickson [of Tods Murray and Jamieson] all papers which appeared to refer entirely to Sir William Fraser's personal business affairs. I have, as we arranged and as the Trustees at their last meeting approved, sent to the National Library a box of papers of historical interest. Many of these had been marked by Macphail

as suitable for presentation to the Library. I have kept a few autographs for my own collection. I have put all the remaining papers into a large box which I propose to hand over to you. The box is here, addressed to you, and can be sent down when you return to Edinburgh. Please deal with its contents as you think proper. They are all in good order and include many interesting papers and some of value, e.g. letters of Scott and of David Hume. Some of them might be suitable for presentation to the Lyon Office or to the Record Office. I suggest that you might select anything which you wish to keep and that you might then pass them on to Balfour-Melville [Secretary of the Scottish History Society]. When he is done with them we can consider as to the disposal of the residue. I think most of them might be destroyed.

I have also laid out for you the green tin box containing Sir William's note-books and diaries. I think these should be preserved by the Trustees. They contain much of the material collected for the Family Histories and many details about Sir W.'s personal life, which it seems a pity to destroy. Among much that is of no importance one finds really interesting things – for example the record of a luncheon at Lady Ashburton's on June 16, 1877, at which Sir W. met Thomas Carlyle, and what Carlyle said to him about Disraeli. Also there are some amusing notes about his quarrels with John Clerk Brodie !

I shall be glad to know that you approve.

You will remember that the boxes of Fraser papers which were removed from Macphail's house after his death are at 66 Queen Street. After you return we shall have to consider how we are to deal with them....

It is clear that the proposed examination of the contents of the nine boxes proceeded only very slowly. In November 1939 it was reported that Innes had at last made a 'preliminary investigation' of certain boxes and two months later the Trustees considered notes by Innes and Dickson, but apparently no action was taken at this point except the disposal of certain printed material.[19] It is hard to relate these proceedings to the existence of a 'catalogue' (consisting only of brief headings) of the contents of eight boxes made in 1953.[20] W.K. Dickson died on 14 July 1949 and his widow handed over some papers to the Trustees, who passed them on to the Library[21] remarking (with unconscious irony in view of what Dickson had written in 1934) that 'my husband had such a strong feeling for keeping records of every kind unbroken'.[22] The other Dickson – Douglas Dickson of Tods, Murray and Jamieson – died in December 1958, but it was W.K.'s widow who made further presentations to the Library – a collection of miscellaneous MSS. brought together by her husband and including some Fraser papers (MSS 3993–8) and yet another transmission in 1955 (5406).

The 'autographs' which Dickson retained for his own collection were probably among the papers presented to the Library by his widow in 1955 (MS 5406). As to 'note-books', the Library did indeed acquire some Fraser notebooks, but quite fortuitously. When Mr Alan Bell wrote to me on 5 November 1968 he stated: 'Fraser material tends to turn up in unusual places. In 1961 Seaton [one of his colleagues in the Library] brought in five small pocket notebooks taken by Fraser on his journeys to muniment rooms. They had been found thrown into his neighbour's garden, perhaps discarded after being stolen: the police allowed us to keep them, and they have been catalogued "subject to any proprietary claim being established". I hope the Trust does not care to establish one!' These note-books, catalogued as MSS 8902–8905, have been used in the present compilation, especially in the section dealing with Fraser's travels.

Besides the Register House and the Advocates' Library, the Lyon Office was regarded as a suitable repository for certain material, and in 1899 the Trustees prepared a list of inventories of title deeds etc. which they presented to the Lyon Office.[23] Other papers evidently found their way to the same repository in successive batches, for in April 1932 Sir Francis Grant, Lyon, gave a receipt for a 'mass of genealogical material ... left by the Trustees from time to time at the Lyon Office'[24] In the Lyon Office I examined a large set of notebooks bearing numbers from xi to clxxxii (with some gaps) which I thought might be Fraser's, but they are the notebooks of an extremely industrious searcher of records who was still operating after Fraser's death. I did discover a number of bundles of Fraser papers. including the correspondence, referred to in an earlier section, about the copies of *Grant* and *Cromartie* disposed of by Sir Bernard Burke's executors and also certain items which throw some light on Fraser's accumulation of material which could assist him in his various activities, e.g.

> Folder titled 'Hamilton of Innerwick etc.' which contains old pedigrees of various Hamilton families, compiled in the 17th and early 18th centuries
>
> 'Mar Peerage: Newspaper extracts 1877–1894'
>
> Bundle titled 'Cavers: Inventory of Writs', including 17th century inventories.
>
> 'Carmichael File' relating mainly to Hyndford Peerage

and containing notes on searches made before
Fraser's time and a Rent Roll of Bangor 1681
Folder containing Genealogy of Maxwells 1742,
Memorandum on Waddells of Crawhill and cognate
families and testimonials for James and David
Baillie and John Wilson 1664
Letter by John Riddell, 12 Oct. 1848, relating to
heraldry of Earl of Dirleton
Pedigree of Elphinstone descent
Pedigree of John Abernethy, Bishop of Caithness, 1727
Pedigrees of Dick family
Folder of 17th century deeds relating to Dicks and
Cunninghams
Bundle of 17th–18th century deeds and notes
Genealogies and writs relating to families of Ramsay
of Abbotshall, Ogilvy of Boyne, Murray of Falahill
and list of heirs of entail of earldom of Moray 1818
'Writs relating to Kers', with pedigrees of Ferniehirst
Volume of pedigrees of Hamiltons and other Clydesdale
families 'in the handwriting of Alexander Deuchar'
[a professional genealogist]
Bundle of pedigrees and other material of Hays of
Alderston, Brisbanes and Maxwells of Terregles
Bundle on Somervilles of Cambusnethan, Lockharts of
Milton etc.
Bundle of notes and pedigrees of 'Hay-Macdougal,
Brisbane, Corbet, Makerstoun'.
'Fife file, Sir William Fraser's collection', including
list of Fife heritors 1845 and notes on Fife families
'Nisbet file', with 17th and 18th century deeds and
a Memoir of Sir John Nisbet of Dirleton
'Miscellaneous File', with notes on various families
in alphabetical order, mainly by Fraser, including
letter by Fraser to James H. Burnett, Esq., W.S.
4 Apr. 1854:–

Dr Sir,
I have devoted two evenings to the Burgie Papers
[Dunbar of Burgie, Forres], and have prepared
rough notes on the evidence recovered and still to
be searched for. Before extending the notes, I
should be glad to have a meeting with you and Sir
William Dunbar, that we may go over some points
which I think important.
As I am confined to the Register House, perhaps
you will not object to favour me with a call there.
I am least engaged between 11 and 12.
Yrs faithfully
W.F.

Bundle titled 'Baillie of Jerviswoode etc.', including

notes of searches, some by Fraser, an 18th century
inventory and a pedigree by Fraser dated 1850.
Bundle titled 'Strachan of Thornton', relating to the
Thornton baronetcy, including a letter from Fraser.
dated 1846, showing that he was engaged on a
claim to this title.

All of the material which I examined in the Lyon Office,
whether or not it came from Fraser, has now been deposited in the Record Office (GD 397).
Seven boxes, with a few unboxed papers, were found
in the Fraser Homes at Colinton in 1964. I made the
following report. with recommendations for disposal of the
material.

1. Letters and papers relating to Fraser's professional work
and his books, including a very few original papers of
pre-19th century dates. This material is in boxes No. 3
4. and the few old papers are in box 3.

    I suggest that the Register House is a very suitable
resting-place for this material, and I hope it will be
accepted if offered.

2. Correspondence of Fraser, mainly of a more personal
nature. This is contained in box 2.

    I suggest that this be offered to the Register House,
with authority to destroy material which is considered to
be of no permanent value.

3. Prints of peerage cases in box 6.

    I suggest that these too should be offered to the
Register House, which may be able to supplement its
existing collection from them.

4. A quantity of photographic plates, contained in box 1.

    It is hard to see any alternative except destruction.

5. A large quantity of portraits and other illustrations from
Fraser's volumes. These are in boxes 5 and 7.

    A few of the illustrations are heraldic, and the
collection might therefore be considered in the first place
by the Lyon Office. The prints of portraits could be
offered to the National Portrait Gallery, though it is
unlikely that many, if any, would be of use to them. The
plates of old buildings etc. are an even bigger problem,
but a print seller might be consulted.

6. Printed material other than peerage cases. This is not
boxed. but it is tied up in a bundle.

    A good deal of this material is probably not deserving
of preservation. as it duplicates matter in published

volumes, but it could be vetted by someone with ready
access to printed books. If the Register House would look
at it that would be admirable; failing that the National
Library might be asked.

7.  A small quantity of facsimiles of documents from Fraser's
    books. Not boxed.

    The obvious resting–place for these would be the
Scottish History Department in the University. where there
is a very substantial bulk of similar material.

I did in fact remove the last group to the Scottish History
Library in the University. Lyon, in a letter dated 12
October 1964, suggested that item 2 should be offered to
the National Library and item 3 to the Lyon Office. with
a view to filling any gaps in its very comprehensive
holding of Peerage Cases.
    After all the migrations which resulted in several
batches of Fraser papers finding homes in various
repositories, five boxes of material which were in the
hands of the Trustees were surveyed for the National
Register of Archives (Scotland).[25] The contents consisted
mostly of papers of dates from the sixteenth century and
had clearly been removed from various collections. and
they included some letters of Sir Walter Scott. The material
was placed on temporary deposit in the Register House in
1972. and in 1983 the terms of the deposit were made
indefinite, with the result that the collection is now among
the Gifts and Deposits (GD 397). The fact that this
material was deposited temporarily in 1972 suggests that
it is to be identified with the papers described by W.K.
Dickson in 1934 and sent by him to Thomas Innes of
Learney but possibly kept by Innes in his own home and
not in the Lyon Office. At any rate, on 23 February 1972
Mr David Scott–Moncreiff reported to me that Lady Lucy,
widow of Thomas Innes of Learney. had handed over to
him Fraser papers which were at her home (35 Inverleith
Row) and which he identified as some of the material
described by W.K. Dickson. The presumption is that these
papers, at this stage lodged in the offices of Tods Murray
and Jamieson, were then surveyed for the Register of
Archives.
    Apart from the MSS which Fraser had accumulated and
the printed items already mentioned, there had been the
question of the disposal of spare copies of the family
histories and other printed material. As to the family
books, copies had originally been allowed to Fraser on the
understanding that they were not to be sold. and the
Trustees decided that it would be improper to sell them
after his death.[26]  They could, however. be given away

and in July 1899, when the Mitchell Library, which had asked in vain for *Buccleuch* at the time of its publication, applied for copies of volumes to complete a set, it was agreed that the Library should receive *Colquhoun, Annandale* and *Elphinstone*[27] The Duke of Argyll, who had all the histories except the recently issued *Elphinstone*, asked for that and got it. [28] There were also prints of Peerage Cases. In April 1940 it was noted that some had gone to the National Library and others to the Register House, but the bulk of them evidently went to the Lyon Office, to constitute a very comprehensive collection. Some engravings and prints were presented by the Trustees to the Scottish National Portrait Gallery in 1931 and a matrix for a seal of Alexander Kennedy of Knockgray was made over to J.W.J. Clark-Kennedy in the same year.[29]

Fraser's bequests had included £3000 for the 'publishing or printing for private circulation or otherwise of such documents as [the Trustees] may think proper with the special object of illustrating the history and antiquities of Scotland'. This enabled the Trustees to give substantial financial assistance, of the order of £2000, towards the publication of *The Scots Peerage*, the first volume of which came out in 1904,[30] and to present the two volumes of *Macfarlane's Genealogical Collections* to the Scottish History Society in 1899 and the *Register of Greyfriars Burials* to the Scottish Record Society in 1902. The volume of *Fraser Papers* which they presented to the Scottish History Society in 1924 represented a fair sample of the varied nature of Fraser's acquisitions: the originals seem now to be among the Fraser Papers in the National Library (MS 90) but the copy of the printed volume in the Register House has corrections in the hand of William Angus, who was Curator of Historical Records at the time the volume was published, which suggests that the papers were once in the Register House; the printed volume itself does not disclose the whereabouts of the papers.

REFERENCES *

Chapter 1
Early Years and Private Life

1    Many of the particulars of Fraser's life were drawn
     from the Memoir prefixed to the Scottish History
     Society volume of *Fraser Papers* (ed. J.R.N. Macphail,
     1924) [hereafter cited as *Memoir*], which used letters
     and other material which cannot now be traced. Most
     of the genealogical particulars have been checked from
     the original Parish Registers.
2    GRS Kincardine, 123.84; MB, i, 4 July 1898.
3    *Memoir*
4    Ibid.
5    GD 397 [the collection surveyed for the National
     Register of Archives (Scotland) as Survey No. 800]
     Box 1, folder 11 (7 Jan. 1838)
6    *Memoir*
7    Ibid.
8    Ibid.
9    GD 39/5/243/40.
10   *Memoir; Edinburgh Directories*; Census Schedules; GRS.
     Edinburgh; the evidence of the places from which
     certain letters are dated.
11   *Memoir*; Census.
12   Census.
13   Information from the late Dr. C.T. McInnes.
14   Register of Deaths; Information from Mr A.D. MacLeod,
     son of John MacLeod; MB. i, 66
15   GD 224/197/1/236; NLS MS 8902.
16   Information from the Minister of St Cuthbert's, per
     Rev. A. Ian Dunlop.
17   *Memoir*
18   MB, i, Dec. 1898.


* Except where otherwise stated, the MSS. referred to are
in the Record Office, H.M. General Register House, in the
categories Gifts and Deposits (GD) and Office Record (SRO).
The Minute Books of the Fraser Trustees (MB) are in the
office of Tods, Murray and Jamieson, W.S. 66 Queen
Street, Edinburgh.

Chapter 2
The Register House

1    SRO 8/62
2    SRO 8/71
3    GD 224/197/1/191; Argyll Papers, bundle 988 (cf. sect-
     ion 8 below)
4    SRO 2/10/310
5    GD 124/15/1833/70; GD 124/15/1833/96;GD 124/15/1839/1
6    Atholl L. Murray, 'The Lord Clerk Register' and Mar-
     garet D. Young, 'The Age of the Deputy Clerk Register
     1806–1928', SHR, liii, 124–93; Margaret D. Young,' "A
     Man of No Common Stamp": Sir William Gibson Craig,'
     Stair Soc. Miscellany Two, 295–315.
7    SRO 2/6. pp. 348–9, 31 Aug. and 7 Sept. 1880
8    Ibid. 350
9    Ibid. 350–53
10   Ibid. 9/197/1–3
11   SRO 5/198
12   SHR, liii, 176
13   SRO 2/6/552–3
14   SRO 7/158
15   SRO 5/195
16   SRO 8/145/13
17   GD 40/9/454/14
18   GD 224/197/6/60
19   GD 40/9/454/20–21
20   GD 40/9/462/25
21   GD 40/9/462/25 and 31; SRO 2/17/38–40 and 9/197/1–3
22   SRO 2/6 pp. 561–3.

Chapter 3
Travels

1    GD 224/197/1/87
2    GD 224/197/1/179–80
3    GD 224/197/1/281
4    GD 237/269/5/6
5    G. Donaldson, Northwards by Sea (2nd edn., 1978), 16–7
6    Memoir, 13–4
7    GD 40/9/454/17
8    GD 39/5/243/14 and 21
9    GD 39/5/243/50 and 57
10   Ibid. 71
11   GD 224/197/1/30
12   NLS MSS 8902–6
13   GD 124/15/1818/1 and 2
14   SRO 8/105/8; NLS MS 8906
15   GD 40/9/454/8
16   NLS MS 8904
17   GD 224/197/1/122
18   NLS MS 5406 fo. 74

19    GD 224/197/1/191
20    GD 224/197/1/179
21    GD 224/197/1/277
22    GD 224/197/1/281 and 295
23    GD 224/197/1/378

Chapter 4
Peerage Cases

1     *Memoir*, p. 12 Much of the evidence about Fraser's
      participation in peerage cases comes from the prints
      of the cases themselves, of which much use has been
      made in this section.
2     GD 39/5/243/1, 2, 4, 14; NRA(S), 800, Box 1. folder 7
3     GD 39/5/243/12
4     GD 39/5/243/48
5     GD 39/5/243/24
6     GD 39/5/243/6, 67
7     GD 39/5/243/63
8     GD 39/5/243/81
9     GD 124/15/1818/1, 2
10    GD 124/15/1839/1
11    GD 124/15/1833/142
12    GD 124/15/1839/1
13    GD 40/9/462/18; 124/15/1847/4, 19, 20, 32
14    GD 124/15/1833/14,70, 127
15    GD 224/197/1/141; 224/197/6/51
16    GD 224/197/6/27 and 30
17    GD 40/9/431/36
18    GD 397, box 2, bdles 4 and 11

Chapter 5
Family Histories

1     GD 224/197/1/12
2     GD 224/197/1/9
3     GD 224/197/3/23x–55
4     GD 40/9/431/34
5     GD 224/197/5/19; MB, i, 6 Feb. 1899
6     GD 224/197/5/19
7     GD 224/197/4/19
8     GD 397, box 1. folder 2
9     GD 40/15/25/1 and 2
10    NRA(S) 859. box 202, bdle 7
11    GD 40/9/431/1
12    GD 40/9/431/2
13    GD 40/9/454/8
14    GD 224/197/1/366
15    NRA(S) 859. box 202, bdle 7
16    GD 224/197/1/1
17    GD 224/197/1/9

18   GD 224/197/1/28
19   GD 224/197/3/10, 39, 55
20   GD 224/197/1/180
21   GD 224/197/1/337
22   GD 40/15/25/2
23   GD 224/197/1/189, 215
24   GD 224/197/1/164
25   GD 220/5/2007(1)
26   GD 40/9/431/30
27   GD 224/197/1/188
28   GD 224/197/1/347
29   GD 224/197/6/24
30   GD 220/5/2007(3)
31   GD 40/9/431/30 and 34; GD 40/9/462/12-3
32   GD 224/197/1/336
33   GD 224/197/2/47
34   GD 224/197/1/48, 95, 105, 126
35   GD 40/9/454/3, 16, 17; GD 40/9/462/21, 26; GD 40/9/431/30
36   GD 40/9/462/15
37   GD 40/9/462/21
38   GD 40/9/462/35
39   GD 40/9/462/36
40   Fraser Papers in Lyon Office, 4 Jan. 1895
41   GD 224/197/3/23x
42   GD 397, box 2, bdle 1
43   GD 397, box 2, bdle 2
44   NLS MS 5406
45   NLS MS 3553
46   GD 224/197/2
47   NLS MS 5406 fo. 65
48   Fraser Papers in Lyon Office
49   GD 40/9/454/3
50   GD 224/197/1/226
51   GD 224/197/8
52   SRO 8/105/8

Chapter 6
HMC

1   Stuart is in the *DNB* and there is an obituary in
    *The Scotsman* on 2 July 1877
2   SRO 2/10/309-12
3   SRO 9/93
4   SRO 9/187/1, 2, 3, 7; SRO 2/6, 449, 551
5   *HMC Report* ii, App. 165
6   GD 220/5/2007 (3-6)
7   GD 40/9/454/19

Chapter 7
'Driving Four in Hand'

1   GD 268/457/4, 5; cf. Gordon Loch, *The Family of Loch* (1934), 138–45.
2   SRO 8/145/9
3   SRO 8/145/10
4   SRO 8/151/3, 4
5   SRO 8/152/1, 2
6   GD 224/197/1/7
7   GD 40/9/431/3
8   GD 40/9/454/13
9   Ibid
10  GD 224/197/3/6x
11  GD 224/197/1/30
12  SRO 8/105/8
13  GD 124/15/1833/70
14  GD 224/197/1/130
15  GD 224/197/1/196
16  GD 224/197/1/245
17  GD 224/197/3/6x
18  GD 124/15/1833/96
19  GD 224/197/1/9 sqq., 217; NRA (S) 859, box 202 bdle 7.
20  GD 224/197/6/14
21  GD 39/5/243/24
22  NRA(S) 859, box 201 bdle 9
23  NRA(S) 859, box 202 bdle 7
24  GD 224/197/1/28, 128; GD 40/9/454/21
25  GD 224/197/1/4 sqq.
26  GD 224/197/1/8
27  GD 224/197/1/50, 185
28  GD 224/197/1/214
29  GD 124/15/1847/20
30  GD 224/197/3/29x
31  GD 224/197/6/64
32  GD 40/9/431/30
33  GD 40/9/454/19
34  GD 224/197/1/215
35  GD 40/9/462/20
36  NLS MS 3553 fos. 30–1
37  GD 224/197/3/4x

Chapter 8
Unfinished projects

1   GD 40/15/25/3 and 40/9/431/1
2   GD 40/9/454/4
3   Ibid. 8
4   GD 40/15/25/3 and 40/9/462/2

5    GD 40/9/431/3
6    GD 40/15/25/3/4
7    GD 40/9/431/26, 30
8    GD 40/9/462/12
9    GD 40/15/25/3(2)
10   GD 40/9/454/24
11   GD 40/15/25/3(3)
12   GD 40/15/25/1, 2
13   GD 40/15/25/3
14   GD 40/9/431/3; 40/15/25/3
15   GD 40/9/462/11
16   GD 40/9/454/13
17   NRA(S) 859, box 202 bdle 4
18   GD 40/9/462/2 and 40/9/431/4
19   GD 40/9/454/1, 2
20   GD 40/9/431/6 sqq.
21   GD 40/15/25/3
22   GD 40/9/454/7, 13
23   GD 40/9/454/13
24   Argyll Papers, bdle 988
25   GD 224/197/1/191
26   NLS MSS 5320-34
27   GD 124/5/1833/35
28   SRO 8/150/3

Chapter 9
The Reckoning and the Rewards

1    GD 224/197/5/19, 224/197/4/3
2    GD 224/197/4/16
3    GD 397, Box 2 bdle 5
4    GD 40/9/431/30
5    GD 224/197/4/37
6    GD 39/5/243/14
7    Ibid. 67
8    Ibid. 78
9    GD 224/197/4/18
10   GD 397, Box 2 bdle 1
11   Ibid. bdle 2
12   Ibid.
13   GD 40/9/462/32-3
14   GD 397, Box 2 bdle 2
15   MB i, 15 June 1898
16   GD 40/9/454/4, 8
17   GD 40/9/462/7/1
18   Ibid. 462/14
19   GD 224/197/3/4x, 224/197/1/416, 224/197/6/55
20   GD 40/9/462/1
21   GD 224/197/1/378
22   Register of Deeds, 2858, p. 196

23　MB i, 27 December 1898
24　University of Edinburgh Court Minutes, 18 Apr. 1898, 13 June 1898, 17 Oct. 1898
25　Ibid. 13 March 1899, 17 December 1900
26　Ibid. 19 July 1901
27　Ibid. 15 May 1899
28　MB ii, 114

Chapter 10
Fraser in Controversy

1　Bruce Lenman, reviewing *The Renaissance and Reformation in Scotland* in *The Scotsman*, April 1983
2　Mark Napier to Lord Napier, 19 March 1879, see below n. 4
3　Prefatory Note to *The Lanox of Auld*
4　Mark Napier to Lord Napier, 19 March 1879: SRA(S), ex bdle 157 of the papers of Col. B.C.A. Napier
5　Mark Napier to Lord Napier, 13 April 1879: ibid. bdle 160. There is more correspondence between Fraser and Francis Napier in NLS MS. 1164
6　Cf. NLS MS 6110
7　GD 220/5/2007 (3–6)
8　NLS MS 5606 fo. 69
9　NLS MS 5312 fo. 70
10　Ibid. 175
11　Ibid. 176
12　Ibid. 179
13　Ibid. 189–91
14　GD 224/197/1/54
15　GD 224/197/1/254–6

Chapter 11
Fraser's Papers

1　Tods, Murray and Jamieson: Paper in Deed Box; Trustees Minute Book. Dec. 1898
2　MB i, 6 Feb. 1899, 18 Oct. 1899
3　MB i. 9 May 1901. 20 January 1913
4　GD 224/197/3/10
5　GD 40/15/25/3
6　GD 397. box 2, folder 1
7　Tods, Murray and Jamieson: Paper in Deed Box
8　MB i. 331–2
9　Ibid., ii, 170
10　MB, 14 July 1931. 12 January 1950
11　Ibid.. i, 91; Livingstone's *Guide*, 35; *SHR* xxvi, 31
12　SRO 5/221, 16 March 1903
13　MB i, 331–2
14　GD 397, box 2, folder 1
15　MB 7 August 1934, 8 August 1934

16  Letter from Alan Bell, Assistant Keeper, 5 Nov. 1968
17  Photocopy of this letter sent to me by Mr David Scott–
    Moncrieff on 23 Feb. 1972
18  MB ii, under date
19  MB iii, 24 November 1939, 15 January 1940
20  Ibid. iii, 336 sqq.
21  Ibid., iii, 25 Oct. 1949
22  Ibid., iii, 327
23  GD 397, box 2, bdle 4
24  MB ii, 11 April 1932
25  GD 397
26  MB, Dec. 1898
27  Ibid., 13 July 1899
28  Ibid., 20 December 1923
29  Tods, Murray and Jamieson: Papers in Deed Box
30  MB i, 166, 274